Foreword by Jonathan T. Gilliam,
Author of *Sheep No More*

SIERRA TWO

A Navy SEAL's Odyssey in War and Peace

by Marc Lonergan-Hertel

SIERRA TWO

A Navy SEAL's Odyssey in War and Peace

To Nancy,
We begin our odyssey
together! I look forward
to completing our mission
together ̬ in this life
and the next.

by Marc Lonergan-Hertel

♡ Marco

Post Hill
PRESS

A POST HILL PRESS BOOK

ISBN: 978-1-68261-732-8
ISBN (eBook): 978-168261-733-5

Sierra Two:
A Navy SEAL's Odyssey in War and Peace
© 2018 by Marc Lonergan-Hertel
All Rights Reserved

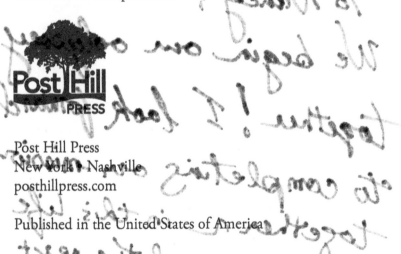

Post Hill Press
New York • Nashville
posthillpress.com

Published in the United States of America

CONTENTS

AUTHOR'S NOTE

Life is what happens while you are making plans or following your dreams. Reality, however, is seldom a movie script as you navigate the challenges before you. In the end, life boils down to just two words: Choice and consequence.

We make our choices, which translate into stepping stones or the distance between our dreams—and sometimes find out that the stone on which we now stand is but yet another in the journey. The consequences of our choices span the spectrum in size, opportunity, and also how they affect the people around us. They prepare us for the next stone with new skills or friends, victories or defeats, humilities or tragedies.

You have never lived until you have almost died. For those who have fought for it, life has a special meaning the protected will never know—until we share it.

—Marc Lonergan-Hertel

AUTHOR'S NOTE

FOREWORD

I remember the first time I met Marc in Panama, on Rodman Naval Base. He was a cross between a classic California surfer dude and a philosopher, and I was a brand-new Ensign straight out of Basic Underwater Demolition / SEAL (BUD/S) training. I had been sent down to Panama for Junior Officer Training while I waited for SEAL Tactical Training to begin, back up in Norfolk, Virginia at Little Creek Naval Base.

Whenever Marc and I talked there was always a deep mutual exchange of life stories and of course some brutal practical jokes. I cannot emphasize the practical jokes enough because you never knew when or where you were going to be a victim. Just like the Pink Panther movies from the 1960s when Inspector Clouseau would come home and out of the blue be sporadically attacked by Cato, these practical jokes were almost an advanced level of unconventional warfare training, and Marc was one of the best at carrying out these covert attacks.

Throughout the years at SEAL Team FOUR, Marc and I continued to work together while he was in the Training Department putting my platoon through various training evolutions. Whenever I saw him it was like meeting up with a best friend or relative that you haven't seen in a long time. We just picked up where we left off and before long the conversations would spin back up and, by that time, enough practical jokes had been carried out (usually with me as the victim) and enough time had passed that we could now sit and laugh about the ridiculous outcomes.

Later, after Marc and I had left the military, the length of time between when we saw each other increased and went from months to years. But when we did see each other, we both had interesting stories about our most recent adventures and how we had each continued to be driven to serve.

Two different paths, yet somewhere along the way, sitting in the open doorway of a BlackHawk helicopter with our knees in the breeze on a rescue mission with our SEAL mentor, Doc Fullerton, we realized that we were not only SEALs, but we were also protectors. Marc's call sign that day was SIERRA-TWO (shorthand for the pilots to recognize the SEALs in the water) and it went on to represent a common theme for us all in our lives: accomplish the mission, and know that you are never far from a strong arm to hoist you out of trouble.

While few people in this world choose to serve anything but their own self-interests, the world is made safer because of men and women that are driven to place their own lives on a shelf and pick up the tools necessary to serve their fellow human beings. Of these few, there is even a smaller number that aren't just called to serve, but they are called to protect. To be honest, I never fully considered my role as a protector until another one of the late night conversations between Marc and I. But it is clear now. Everything that has occurred in my life, intentional or thrust upon me by God, has systematically groomed me as a protector, and the same can definitely be said about Marc.

I consider Marc Lonergan-Hertel my brother, a mentor, and a fellow warrior. If you want to know him like I do, then read SIERRA TWO, *the true story of one man's real world odyssey.* Who knows, maybe you'll discover that you're a protector as well.

- Jonathan T. Gilliam, U.S. Navy SEAL, Federal Air Marshal, Security Contractor, and FBI Special Agent, Author of *Sheep No More: The Art of Awareness and Attack Survival*

PRELUDE: MAN OVERBOARD

*A large wave buries the bow of Seamaster, and I am
exhaling bubbles into the ocean as I try to call for help.
And then I am hit with a distinct sensation.
I can no longer breathe...*

LOCATION: Antarctic Peninsula—Lat/Long: 62.14 South/58.40
West
OBJECTIVE: South Shetland Islands—Potter Cove
DATE: 09 March 2001
AUTHOR AGE: 34

I have my spotlight trained dead ahead.

My mission is to find a path through the ice surrounding
our ship.

The wind and waves of the Southern Ocean are in my face
at 35 knots gusting to 40; the ocean is brutally cold. The seas are
confused, charging toward our polar exploration vessel in mountainous peaks of ocean swell from the west.

Wave heights are at least twenty feet. The air smells fresh and
crisp, as if we are atop the highest mountain in the world. For
a moment I feel transported skyward to that very peak, then the
mix of the brine on the mist of the waves brings my senses back to
sea level.

We have just passed 62 degrees latitude, and there is no longer any landmass to stop the wind, current, and waves on their

circuitous west-to-east journey around the planet. Sir Ernest Shackleton called this area The Screaming Sixties. We are trying not to repeat the misfortunes he encountered on the opposite side of the Antarctic Peninsula when his vessel *Endurance* was trapped and crushed by the same growing fields of brash ice back in the early 1900s.

I am incredulous at the magnitude of the giant walls of water charging at us on what feels like a tiny observation platform. I feel as though I am being sacrificed to King Neptune himself by the vessel *Seamaster*.

I glance back to her captain, who is bathed in the dark red light of the pilothouse. The man at the helm, Sir Peter Blake, has more than six hundred thousand miles racing sailboats through the world's oceans and several world records circumnavigating the planet.

His long, bushy blond hair and scruffy blond mustache are covered in ice as he operates the aft helm. Being outside of the protected cockpit the ice is freezing to his beard. He reminds me of a Viking commander sailing his vessel into battle. Shards of ice stream off the rigging and pass dangerously close to the captain's head, and he returns to the safety of the main pilothouse.

Sir Peter Blake will record the mission we are on tonight as his worst night at sea...and I am catching it right in the face at this moment.

The waves and the wind are not our primary concern tonight, however. After several months at sea, we have traveled further south through King George Sound than any vessel before us.

The year is 2001 and winter is closing in around us. We are in a fight for our lives to escape the crushing ice that has haunted us since we made our expedition's first main objective, Seventy South latitude.

The expedition captain and I nicknamed the objective, calling it *Sierra Two*, which means "MISSION COMPLETE—WE HIT OUR TARGET."

In our expedition planning, we set our objectives in front of us on this epic 35,000-mile journey to make a difference in the world. Our goal is traveling to the pulse points of the planet's health and filming the adventure for Nat Geo Channel and Discovery. We hit our targets on the planet and set our sights on the next. Tonight Sierra Two lies ahead in a protected harbor in the South Shetland Islands, away from the crushing ice fields. It is a daunting objective, as well—a risky one. We are on a mission worthy of the risk, and all of us aboard *Seamaster* have accepted the consequences of failure.

With a gust of wind, the falling snow forms horizontal tornadoes that rotate into my face with gale force. It is completely blinding.

When combined with the violent ups and downs of the moving deck, this dizzying display in front of my face causes vertigo.

Fortunately it is often broken up by a large wall of water, peeled from the ocean by the bow like a fillet. I snap back to my senses. Back to our mission.

A call comes across the frequency on the Marine Band walkie-talkie tied around my neck. *"Lonergan, how are you doing, mate?"* It is Sir Peter from inside the pilothouse, driving the boat.

I hold the radio to my ear. The content of his transmission is distressing, but the sound and tone of his voice are reassuring to me.

"Doing good, Captain." I foolishly refuse to admit my pain.

"Right, then. Best effort, mate," he answers seconds before I get hit by another wall of water in the face.

WHOOSH!

My body gets pounded ruthlessly by a rogue wave that I never saw coming. The bow has submerged under my feet and into the face of a large standing wave, as if I were riding in an elevator with the cable cut away from its fulcrum.

An overwhelming force of inertia overcomes my entire body when *Seamaster* hits a large chunk of ice at the base of the trough. The impact of the wave and the ice throws me from my perch like a toy. With a final effort I key the radio several times before I lose my bearings.

We are not even one-third of the way through our odyssey around planet Earth, and for a moment I fear that I have been cast into the ocean itself. I no longer have the ability to suck precious air into my lungs. I feel a sharp tug from my rescue tether securing me from certain death, my body pounding against the unforgiving hull of the vessel.

I pray the nylon strap holds me from slipping under the metal hull of *Seamaster*.

Breathe!!! my inner voice screams. My body tells me a different story.

To stay alive I calm my heart, try to relax my body, and take the shots against the deck. I force my thoughts to places in my past, visualize the island I swam around as a young boy, practicing my breath holding and swimming like Aquaman. I fast forward to SEAL training and tying knots underwater in a breath-holding drill with my instructors to keep myself from blacking out.

I'm losing the feeling in my hands and struggling to breathe as I try to lift myself back to my station. Back to our mission.

The neoprene mask covering my mouth is saturated with seawater and crusted with ice. It is impossible to breathe. My numb hands find the tether to the ship, but they will not squeeze and pull me to safety, they can only keep me from going over the side. Simple pleasures.

I can't free my hands to rip the bloody mask from my face, and my walkie talkie is choking me as it hangs from my neck. It is almost useless. I cannot speak into it and alert the captain.

As the bow drops, I am dunked into the coldest water on the planet. As it rises I can feel the wind on my face, but I still cannot breathe. I can only do my best to stay alive until my teammates help me.

I remember to be calm and relaxed. *I am not alone.* I am at sea with one of the world's greatest living sea captains and his hand-picked crew on a sailing journey around the world. I need to get back on mission. I need to get back on bow watch and guide us out of the ice.

I feel what can only be a large hand grabbing the back of my survival suit, and with a single heave upward I am pulled back up to my perch like a gaffed fish.

The captain's first mate, Ollie Olphert, lowers me to the icy deck with the help of Janot Pratt and Alistair Moore (Abbo). The three men had advanced to the bow and secured themselves to the rigging above the icy deck and rescued me in almost impossible conditions.

Helpful hands grab the straps of my survival harness to help get the disoriented watchman, me, back on station. Janot and Abbo release their grip on me, as if to signal the rescue operation complete. Abbo's smile is infectious.

I glance at Ollie. No words can express my gratitude to be in the company of such a great team. The large-framed Kiwi has the powerful forearms of a man living a hard life at sea, mostly as a commercial diver on oil rigs. A hard man, with a big, crooked nose and an even bigger smile. There is an enduring spark in his eyes.

The Frenchman Janot puts his face to my frozen nose, his icy beard poking me in the face. His expression is extremely serious. He shows me the end of my rescue tether; the gate of my carabiner was never locked.

Both of us know how precarious the situation had been for me; one wrong twist of my rescue tether could have popped open the spring-loaded opening of my only anchor to the ship. Janot locks it in and looks at me incredulously...and then he laughs with me.

Why is it always the Frenchman that gets to rub it in? I muse to myself.

"Where's your spotlight?" Janot shouts above the roar of the wind and waves.

"I lost it!"

"Here!" Janot clips his light to my harness and gives me the handle. "I'll get it from you when I come out to relieve you. Keep the bow pointed to the sea, not the ice, *mate!*" The Frenchman pats me on the shoulder.

I double-check to make sure I am lashed back into the rigging, then proceed to direct the captain back on course. I find an albatross flying ahead on the edge of the ship's lights moments later and I track its course.

Ollie, the first mate, barks his orders above the wind and waves, "Janot, you go back and get some rest, I'll stay out here with Marco!" He steadies himself on the pitching deck. "When you come back out here, bring Abbo. We go two-man watches tonight!"

Janot and Abbo nod and head back into the warm belly of the vessel.

"Captain, Ollie here!" the first mate says into his radio.

"How we doing, Ollie?" Sir Peter Blake replies.

"All is well. No worries, mate. Lonergan is still on watch."

"Very good, Ollie."

I key in my radio, feeling my hands once again. "Thanks, Captain."

I am secure with the first mate over my shoulder. My teammates have come to my rescue.

We have just escaped the same latitudes that trapped Sir Ernest Shackleton's Endurance almost one hundred years earlier. Sir Peter will document this as the worst night at sea in his life.

That says a lot.

Next stop will be the South Shetland Islands, the final land mass of the Antarctic Peninsula. There, we will get some much-needed sleep before crossing the mammoth waves of the Southern Ocean and making safe harbor in Patagonia. I am mentally preparing myself for the next adventure deep into the Amazon jungle.

We all look forward to the warmer latitudes ahead.

FIVE KNOTS

BUD/S 207—Hell Week
(NSWC Combat Training Tank)
SPRING 1996
AUTHOR AGE: 29

One evolution at a time is the internal dialogue that not only helps me graduate SEAL Training, it will also help me in all of my adventures in the future. I got the mantra from my class leader Sam H. and often repeated it with my class LPO Andy N., my swim buddy Gus, and seventeen original classmates that I graduated with as a part of Class 207. Now there are fifty of us remaining in the class, down from the one hundred and twenty that started.

It is the only mantra I need to repeat to myself over the course of SEAL Training. I still have months and months of this agony in front of me. All I have to do is focus on the mission at hand and not get overwhelmed, not let the demon in my head take over and make me fail…or worse, quit.

One evolution at a time.

I can summarize the rest of my SEAL Training into one evolution: the knot tying test.

My task today is to tie five knots. It is that simple. Tie five knots and advance in my real-world reality TV show called *Make It as a SEAL or Die Trying.*

Today, death is definitely an option for me, because I will not fail this test. Our class had been up for five straight days with little rest and little sleep. Today is a challenge of skill and patience. It is a test to emphasize respect for the water.

Today our challenge is to tie five knots underwater in the NAVSPECWAR Combat Training Tank at a depth of 15 feet. By finishing Hell Week, we are beginning Second Phase, which focuses on building our diving skills. Following behind dive phase we will finish with Third Phase, land warfare skills. We have many more months to go.

One evolution at a time.

In the CTT, the entire class lines up shoulder to shoulder on the edge of the deep pool.

Instructor G is wearing a shortsleeved wetsuit, a black dive mask, and fins. He gives the thumbs up, takes a breath, and descends to a yellow piece of rope that bridges the width of the tank.

The clear water is beckoning.

We already took turns being locked in the chamber of the dive tower and having it flood, open the hatch, and slowly swim to the surface as we release the expanding air in our lungs.

This is an interesting challenge, sitting in a metal ball of space until it is full of water.

Once the room you are in floods, you have to have the composure to calmly open the hatch, swim out into the deep water, and ascend to the surface while you leak bubbles out of your mouth in a steady stream.

Blow and go. Fail to release the air and your lungs can explode from the expanding gas within your chest cavity. Panic and you are toast.

This exercise is second nature for me, but I do not minimize it for one microsecond. I know that water is my best friend...or my worst enemy, even a teaspoon of it.

Below the surface, 'G' is hurrying me along with an arm signal that punctuates a look in his eyes. It is an expression that says, *"Hurry the fuck up."*

I am wearing my tan UDT swimmer shorts and I have a twenty-inch piece of thin manila line in my right hand. I hit the water, adjust to the chilly temperature, and relax my muscles. I am simulating tying remote underwater charges to one central line of Det Cord, a practice that began in WWII. Nothing in this exercise has changed since then, not even the type of shorts I am wearing.

Begin to save air, I tell myself.

I do a required somersault in the water near the surface and do not let my feet touch the side of the tank, then kick myself down to the awaiting instructor.

Instructor G is holding onto the extended yellow rope with both hands and facing the direction he wants me. Directly in front of him, face to face.

I grab the yellow line, called a "Trunk Line," and square off.

He releases his right hand and taps on the line, then makes the number one with his index finger, the signal for me to tie my first knot.

Easy, I think to myself. *A bowline.*

I perform the task and the instructor checks the knot and gives me a thumbs up. I'm supposed to kick to the surface, take a breath and then return for the second knot. I stay on the bottom and nod to the instructor for the next. He takes the challenge.

He raises two fingers.

I move to tie knot number two, a square knot.

I place my white manila perpendicular to the taut yellow rope, bring it around from down under, and tie the two ends of the manila as if capturing the yellow nylon keeping my instructor from floating to the surface.

Two ends left over right, then right over left. Done.

Instructor G checks it quickly and approves, then holds up three fingers.

I look above and see a shit-ton of faces glaring down at me from the surface.

I get distracted for a second and forget what the third knot is. *Think, Marco!*

My instructor gets impatient and shakes the yellow line vigorously. Through his dive mask he says *"Tie the fucking knot, idiot."* He holds up three fingers again.

Oh yeah, a bowline.

Instructor G is pissed. He shakes the line. It's supposed to be a Becket's Bend knot.

I get the manila line over the yellow and then forget the secret code of tying a bowline.

Around the tree and then through the rabbit hole.

The instructors bring down another student who lines up on my right shoulder. The pair goes through the numbers.

I relax and start to feel the breathing demon swell in my chest and into my brain. I take a puff of air from my lungs and inflate my cheeks, then swallow the air. This action helps avoid a laryngeal spasm. It is a bodily function that triggers your brain to make your body gasp for air. The larynx flaps back and forth in the spasm, and if you repress it, as one would do on a breath hold underwater, the resulting spasm sounds like a croaking frog.

That's what happens to the student next to me. He forgets how to tie his knot. Poor guy goes into a spasm and I hear the croaking frog come from my classmate's throat.

He is done.

With a *whoosh*, he is gone, back to the surface.

I get the line shake, cross eyebrows, and bug eyes from my instructor. All of a sudden I hear the instructor start to croak.

I take another puff of air into my cheeks and swallow, then start cycling air from my lungs into my cheeks like bellows. I pretend I am breathing.

This is super dangerous, as I trick my brain into thinking I am taking in air. Although the action suppresses the spasm, I can pass out, and eventually will, but I buy myself precious time.

Puff in...puff out.

Whoosh! My instructor goes to the surface.

Quickly, another instructor descends. It is Instructor P, the second phase lead dive instructor.

Oh shit.

He grabs the taut yellow rope and bends it into the shape of a horseshoe in front of me.

Tie the fucking knot! he says with his body language. His eyes say *DROP, Hertel!*

I tie a bowline again and totally blow the Becket's Bend.

Instructor P simply checks the knot and taps it.

I untie it, and instead of four fingers, he punches me in the chest, then gives me a friendly "OK" hand signal. His eyes tell me everything; *Don't worry about the fourth or the fifth knot...you pass the evolution. But I am going to crush you as soon as you get to the hardtop.*

I swim up to the surface as my LPO jumps in and does his forward flip underwater.

I get a breath of precious air at the surface, catching the smell of chlorine and a fart from Andy as he crop dusts me. I start pumping out push-ups as soon as I climb out of the pool.

There is a lot of symbolism to this rite of passage as a frogman today. Years from now I will train Jacques-Yves Cousteau's youngest son, Pierre-Yves (then 19), in the same breath hold techniques to survive underwater. The patience and the humility of this evolution, as well as my mischief, defines a cadence and internal monologue I develop for myself to succeed and eventually earn class honorman for BUD/S 207. It is with homage that I know the true honorman is each of the members of our class at graduation, especially the leaders.

At the conclusion of training, I get to select my SEAL Team. I choose SEAL Team Four to pursue my dream as a sniper in the jungles of South America.

I am ready for the next evolution.

Doc

Breeze

Honduras, Rio Abajo—
Tegucigalpa

IN GOD'S HANDS

Soto Cano Air Base
Latitude/Longitude: 14.38N, 87.61W
Description: Soto Cano Air Base, Honduras
JTF-Bravo—SEAL Team Four/Charlie Platoon (SOCOM)
YEAR: 1998
AUTHOR AGE: 32

I open my eyes underwater and through the brown, tea-colored water make out the shape of the woman and baby. I stay underwater and swim in behind her. My large swim fins propel me in dolphin kicks.

I make a swallowing motion with my throat, using the free-diving technique I learned early on.

I override the annoyance of breathing and settle into a dolphin kick as the dark shape of the woman comes into better focus.

The water is stained brown from the mud and waste, but it offers enough clarity this far downstream to make out the mother's face underwater. She looks to the surface, the skin on her face illuminated by the sun hitting the water only inches above her.

She is holding up her child with everything she has. The mother has the peaceful look of an acceptance of death on her face as her hair stands up straight above her.

Her descent has begun and is halted by me coming up from the depths behind her.

I get my arm under her right armpit and her cotton shirt brushes my face. I kick up, settling her above my hip and bringing her horizontal to the surface with the child cradled on her chest.

Her body makes a good boat, and I get my face above water and kick to shore, sucking in precious air.

Holding this woman and child, I am aware of the feeling of bringing a life into this world. There is something powerful in capturing the mother and child in their descent and swimming us upward to life.

The moment is etched in my mind as if it is a photograph that I take through the aperture of my unprotected eyes. It is a moment that moves beyond imagery and into a feeling that fills a void in my heart and my soul.

Once safe on the dike, I learn the name of the first little girl that I save that day. Her name is Esperanza. Hope.

"Sierra-One, Sierra-One…this is Sierra-Two—over."

"Go ahead, Breeze. This is Doc."

"Roger, Doc, I'm feet-dry on the riverbed, five hundred meters at your twelve o'clock."

"I just did, Breeze. Pilot has your marking with orange VS-17 panel. Over." My platoon chief confirms they have me in their line of sight. "Roger, Sierra-One. Sierra-Two ready for extract."

Doc double-keys his radio transmit button to give me an affirmative. I wipe the blood off of my saturated camouflage uniform and hear a break again.

"How many did you get, Breeze?" Doc asks me over the crackling radio static.

"Just two, Doc…" I take my fins off and stow the soft nylon fabric signal panel in my right cargo pocket. I can't get the smell of blood and human waste out of my nostrils. Doc comes back over the net.

"Sierra-Two—Sierra-One. Be advised that gives us our first two souls today. Over."

I double-key my mike in response.

My gaze is fixed on the slow-flying Blackhawk helicopter closing in on my position. We are in a wide canyon between two large mountains in the path of what used to be a narrow river, now a complete deluge. Waves on the brown river peak to large whitecaps from the rush of the brown, mud-stained torrent of rainwater.

Doc extends his head out of the port side of the bird and looks below the aircraft as I talk to him. The helicopter is down below the treetops and following the course of the whitewater rapids towards me. Sierra-Three, one of our SEAL officers, Jonathan Gilliam, is behind him pointing to someone in the water.

"Roger that, Doc." I key my radio and speak into the PRC-112 ground-to-air radio as my Platoon Chief, Doc Fullerton, jumps out of the open door of the low flying helicopter.

Doc has a swim fin in each hand. The aircraft looks to be flying at forty knots and at an altitude of forty feet when he makes a snap decision to make a rescue.

The headset he is still wearing gets ripped from his curly blond hair. The black cord that connects him to the aircraft radio system had reached its maximum length and snapped back inside the airframe.

Doc's head is jerked back slightly, but he maintains a perfect, feet-first entry into the water. There is a powerful spray of water from the helicopter rotor wash at the moment he hits the surface of the putrid river. The pilot and co-pilot flare the aircraft as it closes in on me, and the tail almost dips into the tops of the waves before it levels off.

Out in the river, Doc hunches his back as he puts his fins on in the water about one hundred yards away, then makes his way over to another set of victims of the hurricane floodwater. He has a mother and a child in his grasp and he swims in powerful strokes with the two of them as the helo comes into a hover over my head and then shifts over to my right side only inches away.

I put my hands through my fin straps and walk into the shallows towards Doc as the bird touches down on the muddy beach.

I wade out to into the eddy that I used earlier and help my swim buddy guide a heavy woman and her child past the rocks and up onto the shore.

Doc takes his fins off in the shallow water and looks at Sierra Three, who is urging us to get in the aircraft.

"That's two more souls, Breeze," he says. He jumps out of the water and flops onto the awaiting rescue platform like a dolphin. Doc and I are completely in our element.

"There's so many, Doc. How do we choose which ones to save?"

"Go on your lead, Breeze. Look for the single hands to the sky, those are the moms. The rest of them are in God's hands."

In my most difficult times in the years to come, after my time in the SEALs with Doc, I will remember what we did that day, and I will remember that girl.

I end up training Special Forces commands with Doc throughout Central and South America. I specialized in training the sniper teams, and collectively we specialized in jungle warfare and riverine ambushes.

It was the closest thing to combat as I knew it from the stories of the Vietnam veterans when I was growing up as a boy in Scituate, a coastal town in Massachusetts.

Throughout my deployments south, my time as a SEAL is everything I hoped it would be.

At thirty-two-years old, I thought it would be the pinnacle of my accomplishments, but I quickly found it was merely a stepping stone to qualify me for a real-world adventure in times of peace, and later in times of war.

THE ODYSSEY BEGINS: CALYPSO

The Cousteau Society Expedition Warehouse
Chesapeake, Virginia
SEPTEMBER 2000
AUTHOR AGE: 34

Ollie Olphert is waiting for me in Jacques Cousteau's expedition warehouse in Chesapeake, Virginia. Sitting behind a desk that he dwarfs with his forearms, behind a pile of ocean charts and scrolls from various regions of the planet, is a troll of a man who reminds me of...Shrek.

He removes his broken wire frame reading glasses and glances up. His intense blue eyes stare at me as he speaks with a characteristically strong Kiwi accent.

"You the bloke from the Navy SEALs?"

"Yes, sir," I answer.

"Right, mate. You're Hurr-tell?"

"Yes, sir, I am," I answer again, surprised by the sound of my name spoken with the Kiwi inflection, as well as the familiarity this man has with my name.

"Right, but I'm not a sir. That distinction belongs to the captain. I'm Ollie, First Mate to Sir Peter Blake. We heard you might be coming in."

Ollie shifts the broken spectacles with the bridge taped in his Shrek-like hand and replaces them on the crest of his bulbous nose, maintaining his steady gaze. "Can you read a chart?" he asks.

"Sure can, Ollie."

"Good, help me find Antarctica. All I see is the bloody Nile River, here. Can you stay for a bit?" His way of speaking makes it less of an invitation and more of an order.

"Sure can, Ollie."

"Good, mate. There's a bunk in the yellow submarine over there. Sleep there. It'll be a long night." He pauses. "I'm looking for charts used by Sir Ernest Shackleton from his Antarctic expedition aboard the *Endurance*. Cousteau had it in his records here somewhere."

Beyond his tone, I instinctively know that the New Zealander faces something important, something that involves me.

I have been on a journey throughout my life to get me here, to this moment. I have completed twelve years of active duty in the US military, first as a Force Recon Marine, finishing as a SEAL sniper in South America. It was my platoon chief, Doc Fullerton, who found out about this opportunity. The captain chosen to replace the late Jacques-Yves Cousteau, Sir Peter Blake, is searching for someone who can dive the ice shelf of Antarctica and scout a three thousand-mile expedition in the Amazon Jungle—alone.

I am a perfect fit for the mission…if I get the opportunity.

I am getting shivers up my spine at the mention of Sir Ernest Shackleton. The captain and his crew were stranded on the Antarctic Peninsula after their ship was crushed by the ice shelf in the same region as Seventy South latitude, in the early 1900s.

Ollie snaps me out of my haze. "Marco, let's go, mate. We have a lot of work to do. It's a 35,000-mile journey the captain is planning. We have to focus on the first 15,000 if you're up for it."

"Roger that, Ollie." I do not yet fully realize it, but I have just made a spur-of-the-moment decision that will change my life.

I look to the old submarine in the back of the warehouse. It is the same submarine that inspired the Beatles' song, "Yellow Submarine," in the 1960s.

"Who's Sir Peter Blake, Ollie?"

"You haven't heard of him, mate?" Ollie queries, slightly incredulous. "Sir Peter is a New Zealand yachtsman with over 600,000 miles at sea. He won the 1989–90 Whitbread Round the World Race, held the Jules Verne Trophy from 1994 to 1997 by setting the fastest time around the world as co-skipper of ENZA New Zealand, and led his country to successive victories in the America's Cup."

"Where is this expedition going?"

Ollie adjusts the broken reading glasses on his face and looks up at me with the serious look of a first mate about to launch on a dangerous journey with his captain aboard a purpose-built sailing ship.

He is not smiling when he answers me, nor does he break eye contact. "Seventy South, mate.

"Doc Fullerton told me you were mirroring Ernest Shackleton's expedition," I probe.

"Yeah, mate. We'll be transiting to the same latitude that his ship *Endurance* was crushed in the ice."

I join my new friend in sifting through all of the old nautical charts on the table. I can feel that this is a friendship I will have to earn every day that I work under his command.

I find a chart of the Antarctic Peninsula. It is brittle and discolored. The date on the chart is 1910.

I let Ollie handle it. When his rough hands prove too cumbersome on the parchment, I take over. I unfold it over the top of a large scroll of a map mounted on old canvas. It is the chart JYC (Jacques-Yves Cousteau) used for his Nile expedition.

The scroll unrolls to reveal the Nile in its entirety. I see the city of Khartoum on its surface before I use it as a cushion for the Antarctica chart.

Ollie uses a fat finger to indicate Cape Horn, the southernmost point of South America. "The expedition starts here, in Tierra del Fuego."

"The Land of Fire, in Patagonia."

"Doc Fullerton said you could speak Spanish." Ollie smiles at me. "Congratulations, you just passed the test."

"I just translated three of the easiest words in the language, Ollie," I say, smiling back.

"Well, that's three more than I know, so you passed." Ollie laughs and slaps me brutally hard on the right shoulder. It is the first time of many that he numbs my entire arm with his brutish strength and enthusiasm.

I can tell immediately that Ollie is a man who truly lives in the moment. He has seen death stare him in the eye many times. I can tell he appreciates life with a zeal unknown by many. Right now, he is truly living in Patagonia and sailing the Southern Ocean as he traces the chart. I feel viscerally that this is not a trivial pursuit we are engaged in at the moment.

"Shackleton sailed *Endurance* down the eastern shores of the Antarctic Peninsula," Ollie continues. "His goal was the South Pole. His ship was trapped in the ice in the same region we are going. He never made it further south."

"That ship was crushed and he and the crew drifted on the ice. Did they survive it?"

"Yeah, mate, they survived. Had to put down their sled dogs for food, then lived for months on seals they caught on the drifting ice flows. They eventually sailed a dory out to South Georgia Island and they all lived."

"Trapped in the ice, Ollie. That's friggin' nightmare stuff."

"Not with Sir Peter Blake. He secured a polar ice yacht with the help of Madame Cousteau. That's why I am here. The vessel is called *Seamaster*, an icebreaker built to retract her rudders and keel. If she gets trapped, she sits on the ice like a house."

"Sounds like a polar spaceship."

"Yeah, well the captain said we need a SEAL along on the journey. I need a dive buddy under the ice once we make our destination." Ollie squints at me. "We wanted Doc, but sounds like he has other things going on, and wants to retire first. He said you fit the bill."

"Aye, Ollie I'm about to re-enlist. I have an opportunity to try out for Dev Group, or work with the dolphin program, so I am evaluating."

"No promises here. I can't hire you. Sir Peter will give you a test to join the crew. It'll be out in New Zealand where the vessel is under preparations for the journey."

"Is the journey just to Patagonia and Antarctica?"

"No, mate. First it's Seventy South, then the Amazon jungle, then the Northwest Passage, then the South Pacific."

"I'm your man!"

"Hmmm, right then," Ollie says skeptically. "Can I trust you with my life under the ice, mate?"

"Yes, sir."

"Well then, we will just have to see, won't we?"

"Aye, Ollie."

Back at the Teams, Doc has me working at the SEAL Team Four Training Cell teaching the SEAL Hunter program to our deploying platoons, a special program with our counterparts at TF-160 Helicopter Squadron.

I don't have official leave time from the unit to stay with Ollie at the Cousteau warehouse, but Doc has me covered to disappear from the command for several days to make my life decisions.

I love this guy.

On our final night in Virginia, we go to work on a couple of songs back at his house. I play guitar and Doc plays his harmonica.

Doc pours whiskey into two old coffee cups as we sit next to a roaring fire and raise our glasses. Doc issues the toast.

"Alright, Breeze, here it goes," he says. He raises his right hand and sights me in over the top of his mug. "I'm proud of you, Breeze. I'll be watching out for you while you're out there."

"Aye, Senior Chief. Thank you for having my six…always," I answer my platoon chief, friend, and mentor.

We raise our mugs and drink the Crown Royal whiskey, savoring the moment before I jump on a flight to Auckland, New Zealand, to meet Sir Peter Blake and the crew of the vessel *Seamaster*.

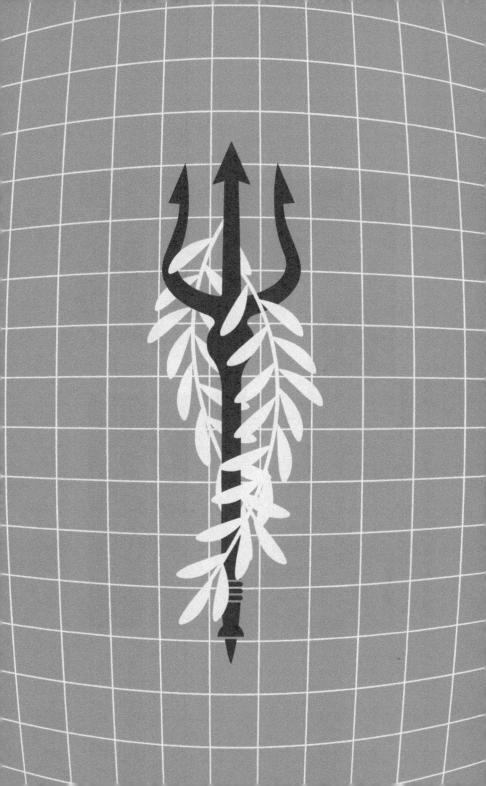

Auckland, NZ

THE TOAST

Bayswater, New Zealand
Bayswater Yacht Club, Sir Peter Blake Avenue
OCTOBER 2000
AUTHOR AGE: 34

The tall captain gestures at me to sit. I settle into a settee in *Archangel's* main salon, and Sir Peter Blake takes two glasses from a bar near the galley.

We have just completed my test. Of all the sailors in the world, I have the chance to make his crew of four.

What does one the world's best sea captain's do to test a former SEAL for a spot on his crew?

He talks with my platoon chief. Then he tells me to take him by Zodiac boat across the turbulent waters of the Hauraki Straights. I had only one directive—keep the captain's shoes dry. It was not an easy task, but his feet are dry on a windy day. It took everything I had as a coxswain to navigate the eighteen-foot rigid hull inflatable in the troughs of the large waves, and avoid the wispy tops of the whitecaps. Sir Peter watched my every move. Only an experienced waterman would pass this test.

The captain is a practical man, and he is only interested in action.

Now that we are in his personal sailboat, he is much more relaxed, and interested in conversation.

"Doc told me a story about you two in Honduras. I didn't want to hear the chest thumping stories, mate, so he told me about a human story. He told me about Hurricane Mitch. He said that changed you."

The captain picks out something to pour into the glasses. I am busy absorbing the moment, looking at the well-lit cabin with dark wood accents everywhere, and books—books in every nook and cranny.

Sir Peter pulls a nautical chart out from a stack of old parchments and weatherbeaten maps of the world. This particular chart is the same one Ollie and I discovered at the Cousteau warehouse. It smells familiar to me, like old paper and wetsuits. The captain picks up a magnifying glass designed for reading charts. It has a dark mahogany handle about six inches long, with a pointed end at the bottom of the handle.

Sir Peter hands me a partially filled glass of liquor and speaks to me in an extremely calm and measured tone as he uses the wooden handle of the glass to trace a path from New Zealand to Cape Horn at the southern tip of Argentina, down to Antarctica, up through the Amazon Jungle, then over the top of Canada near the North Pole, down through the Philippine Islands, circles in the islands of the South Pacific, and ends back in Auckland. With one pass, he covers over 35,000 nautical miles.

The great sea captain looks right through me, "Our mission, Mr. Lonergan, is to plan and execute an expedition around the planet, make a difference, and come out alive. Are you in?"

I start to lift my right hand and answer the toast, but he stops me with his free hand.

"No, mate, that's not how it's done. Aboard this boat, we toast with the right hand up higher, like this." He lifts my glass. "This is the captain's toast. The sea captains of old would meet before a long journey and toast eye to eye, with the right hand holding the glass just below eye level. It meant that they would meet again in this life…or the next." Sir Peter levels his glass and looks into my eyes as if he is aiming a rifle.

"So I offer a toast to our journey, Mr. Lonergan. May we complete it together…in this life or the next," Sir Peter lifts his glass with his right hand and shifts it to its proper configuration, just below eye level. He never breaks his gaze; a powerful gesture that moves me deeply.

The eyes of my captain are cold blue, like the eyes of the great white albatross he chases. They are the deep-water color of the ocean that peels off the surface and curls away from the moving bow of a vessel, a color only blue water sailors know from experience, but one easily imagined by anyone with an adventurous soul. His eyes have the glow of the mystical guardian of the next passage. The comfort of a mentor.

I toast him with my right hand and sip the strong cognac, staring at the man who will take me to the Southern Ocean and beyond, a man I will trust with my life, and in return offer my own if necessary.

"Aye, Captain…in this life or the next."

Though he does not say so, and no longer needs to, I know that I have passed yet another test and have come aboard.

Sir Peter gets down to business. "Our first objective is here, King George the Sixth Sound. The ice is melting here and we will go further south into the polar ice shelf than any vessel in history."

He traces to the western shoreline of the Antarctic Peninsula and circles a large bay near the South Pole with the handle of the magnifying glass. "This is our first objective. Seventy degrees south latitude."

"Seventy South, that's what Ollie told me back in Virginia."

"Seventy South, mate."

"Ollie and I called it, Sierra Two, a call-sign I used back in my SEAL Team days with Doc Fullerton on a rescue mission. It became a codename between Doc and I for making a difference in this world."

"Then that is what we will name our first objective, mate. Sierra Two."

Sir Peter places a finger on a city on the map near the written words, Tierra del Fuego. "You'll be flying out to Patagonia ahead of *Seamaster*. We'll pick you up there. Be a good lad and meet the Discovery Channel film crew and have provisions ready for us to make for Seventy South."

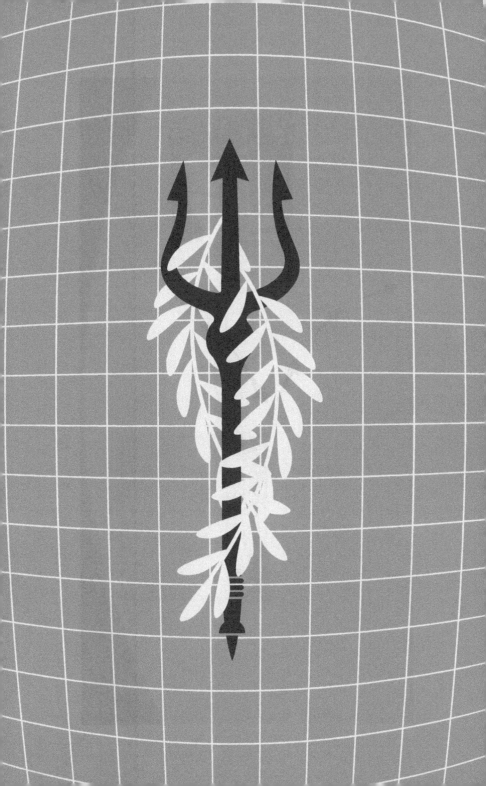

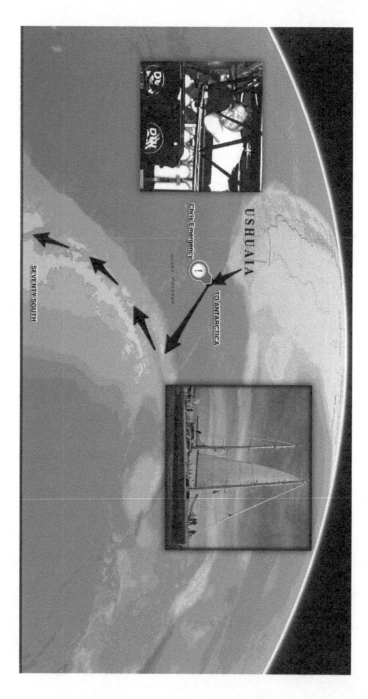

TO ANTARCTICA

The Southern Ocean, Antarctic Peninsula
JANUARY 2001
AUTHOR AGE: 34

Our team is in the process of sailing from Cape Horn as *Seamaster* makes her way toward Seventy South. We are almost five hundred nautical miles north of Trinity Island, on the northern tip of the Antarctic Peninsula. Our objective is the ice cliffs of King George VI Sound, another 1,200 miles to the south. This frozen bay down near the South Pole has never been navigated by vessel until now. No one has ever reached this deep into the Sound.

This year the reports say the ice has melted all the way to the latitude of seventy degrees south.

My captain is on a mission to pull up on the ice shelf at the specific latitude below the cliffs and give a streaming satellite report back to a United Nations Environmental Program conference in Europe. Omega Watches is sponsoring the expedition, and the Cousteau Society, captained by Madame Francine Cousteau, has helped him secure this special vessel.

Sir Peter knows there is only a small window of time to make the distance and hightail it back to the safety of Trinity Island, the last safe harbor off the northern tip of the Antarctic Peninsula, as *Seamaster* heads back home. Trinity is considered out of the 'frozen zone' and Sir Peter *must* get *Seamaster* back to Trinity before the ice of Antarctica freezes us in. With a maximum hull speed of ten knots, every minute counts down here.

With a Discovery Channel film crew on board and Chris, our expedition sponsor, the team and I are doing everything possible to prepare to document the amazing nature and wildlife by diving, climbing, and flying in this remote wilderness.

I spend most of my time during the transit when not on watch in a secret fort I built over the dive gear. The room smells like neoprene and diesel fumes. It is the smell of a frogman's adventure.

It is the long, steady miles of the journey that leave me with many hours of thoughts and reflection. These moments can be a wonderful blessing or a mariner's curse.

To me, it is much like the mind games I experienced at BUD/S where the inner demons come out and bite you if you are not mentally strong.

Earlier on the voyage, I am called out of my fort by Ollie for a celebratory dinner at the captain's table. All hands on deck.

With calm winds and following seas, some 100 miles south of Patagonia, the captain chooses this moment to have a party to commemorate the journey and honor our friend Chris, who has helped make the trip come together along with Omega. Chris is the founder of America True team for the America's Cup race in recent years. He is also one of the developers behind various tech devices. He and his son joined us earlier in Patagonia for diving and expedition prep and we all enjoy Chris's continued presence with us on this first leg. He will be sailing with us until we rendezvous with a cruise ship on the northern tip of Antarctica.

Pete had Janot haul a lamb carcass down from the rigging. Unbeknownst to me, they had raised it high above the vessel since leaving Tierra Del Fuego in reference to the sailing tradition of old to preserve and naturally salt their meat.

As we dine on the succulent meat, fresh bread from our onboard breadmaker, and a beautiful bottle of wine, our guest Chris decides not to chew his food properly.

A piece of meat gets stuck right above his epiglottis and obstructs 80 percent of his breathing.

He goes into a choking fit out at sea and in the middle of nowhere.

Oh shit.

Recognizing the situation as chairs and plates start flying in the salon, I assess the fact that I have been dubbed the ship's medic.

The role is traditionally filled by Doc Trevor, a surgeon from New Zealand with years of experience as Sir Peter's medic on his round-the-world adventures. Doc Trevor and I built the ship's medical kit in Auckland before I cut out to Patagonia. Doc Trevor had left us in Ushuaia and flown home.

This leaves me holding the med bag.

"Lonergan! Do something!" the captain shouts.

Oh shit.

I assess his situation. First of all, he is a big man, about the same girth as New Jersey governor Chris Christy. His face is discolored but not purple. He is holding his hands to his throat but is making gasping noises.

He can breathe! Good.

If he keeps moving it can be a total obstruction in a second though. I have to act.

I try to perform the Heimlich maneuver but there is not enough blockage to clear it properly. I can barely get my arms around him. I end up sitting him down on a bunk close by.

"Don't panic, Chris, you can make it worse."

I hand him a waste bucket and he retches fluids into it.

"Pete called Doc Trevor, they said to wait to see if it clears, and try to drink a Coca-Cola."

Chris nods.

"It may not clear on its own, Chris. Tell you what, we'll give it ten minutes, and if it doesn't work itself out, we will go to plan B. Just don't make it worse."

Chris's eyes give me a look that asks, *"What's Plan B?"*

"Wait here," I say.

I keep an eye on him, and ten minutes later I walk out and return with the ship's shop vac.

"Oh no," he gasps.

"Oh yes."

I hand him the business end of the black plastic tube without any of the end tips. "Wrap your lips around this and make a seal. I'm going to flip it on and hope for the best."

Chris gives it his best effort.

I flip on the vacuum.

SSHHHHHOOOOOOOPPP!

Success!

I check out with the captain and head back to my bunk in the dive locker. I am feeling a little seasick. On the way to the stern I poke my head out of the ship's pilot house. Alistair is at the helm with Janot, both wearing their survival suits and deck boots.

The sailors are watching the main sail and discussing the trim and her course as the waves of the Southern Ocean have grown at least twenty feet in height in a matter of an hour.

No wonder I am feeling queasy!

The ship catches a steady wind gust of twenty-five knots and heels to port. *Seamaster* increases her speed to twelve knots in the large ocean swells. The action around me is intimidating.

We have five days of sailing the open waters through the Furious Fifties before we make it to the Screaming Sixties.

God help me.

Blugghh.

The nautical miles of Antarctica pass under *Seamaster's* belly as the days turn into weeks, the weeks into one month at sea since we left Patagonia. The trip south is only eventful when we pull into a cove and get a good day of diving under the surface with the wildlife, or I get to fly my paraglider (unpowered) from the tops of mountains and film with my helmet camera for the program.

I spend many nights going over charts and maps with Sir Peter. There is one night off of Port Lockroy that stands out above the many nights I spent anchored in icy coves of the Antarctic Peninsula with him.

Odd as it is, we take the time to plan the Amazon leg of the journey together on this particular night. Ollie often joins us with the old charts he dug up at the Cousteau headquarters, but tonight it is just the captain and me.

"How do we tell the story of the Amazon in your opinion, Mr. Lonergan?" the captain asks.

I just finished pouring a hot cup of tea for him, just as he likes it.

I sit next to him in the main salon of *Seamaster* and hold a warm mug of tea in my cold hands. They are still purple from a dive we made earlier in the day to film penguins.

"Aye, captain, we either follow Teddy Roosevelt's route to the south or Cousteau's route to the north."

"No mate, I mean what is our objective. Down here we have Seventy South. It's a geographic pinpoint location on the map, but it represents much more than that."

"I agree, Sir Peter, it is much more than that. Seventy South is our objective, but what is our mission? This needs to be for a higher purpose than simply making it to a spot on the map."

"Right, mate. Explorers measure themselves in latitudes, minutes, and seconds. Our purpose is greater than that."

"Doc Fullerton and I used to use our old call signs as a way to measure our success. As a sniper I would call back to him with 'Sierra Two' as a signal that I hit my target."

Sir Peter listens intently but makes no comment.

"It turned into a code that meant 'MISSION ACCOMPLISHED' when we were in the heat of the battle." I take a sip of my tea. "The way I see it, Seventy South is our Sierra Two."

"No mate, it is not," my captain says. "Our mission is to make a difference, mate. Most people say things like 'Why bother.' My answer is that it's too important not to, Mr. Lonergan."

"I agree, Sir Peter."

"We have some of the biggest corporations in the world supporting us to make a difference with our journey, but there is something deep inside that I can't describe. To anyone. Not even myself."

"That's why Doc and I simply say "Sierra Two." Mission accomplished for us means we are doing something greater than ourselves. We learned it after a Hurricane in Honduras. It means we are the guardians on the wall, keeping others safe."

Sir Peter nods his head, "We're doing this so we can help people fall in love with these places on Earth that are so important. In doing that, we are the guardians on the wall."

"That's it, Sir Peter. Exactly."

"So, it leaves the question, Mr. Lonergan. What is Sierra Two for us in the Amazon?"

"I don't know the answer to that, *Capitan*," I answer, using the Spanish word for captain.

"I think the first challenge will be putting it on a map. Following Roosevelt or following Cousteau."

"That is a massive challenge, Mr. Navy SEAL. I hope you are up for it when it presents itself."

"I have been training my entire life for this challenge, *Capitan*."

It is now February in the year 2001. *Seamaster* must be out of Antarctica before the end of March.

To fight the demons of a long transit at sea, aboard *Seamaster* I dig into my fort in the dive locker to sleep and to read when we are underway and I am not on bow watch. I posted a picture on the bulkhead of the ship that forms the aft wall of my fort. The wall is actually the stern of the icebreaker. It is not a gratuitous picture of a surfer girl in a thong bikini; it is simply a silhouette shape of a woman laying on her side, looking out to sea.

The photo is shot from behind as she is framed by the sunset, her head propped in one arm, her long hair flowing down to the sand.

I dig it because it shows the timeless form of the female with all of her curves. She is the forever girl. She represents the magic of the female form to me.

This photograph of the woman inspires the thoughts of returning from a long journey to a warm bed and a warm companion.

She inspires me to someday have a wife and a family to come home to.

So far the call to adventure and the twists and turns of life have kept me from that reality. Still, I spend my time dreaming of the day it will happen.

The propellers churn the ocean below my bunk, the spinning prop shafts whirring to a familiar frequency, being driven by the roar of the diesel engines.

One morning, the whirring stops and there is silence in the dive locker. *Seamaster* has reached her next destination, and it is time to go to work.

Ollie enters the dive locker and lifts the blanket covering my fort.

"Seventy South, mate. Let's get the dive gear ready, Lonergan!"

Ollie and I start pulling out dry suits, dive fins, and masks before the dive compartment begins to cool down from the engine heat.

The temperature outside the hull of *Seamaster* is frigid, the water temp is the coldest that saltwater can physically attain.

The two of us are interrupted by Janot.

"Hey, Ollie, Marco. The captain, wants to speak with all of us. We're five minutes latitude north of our bloody objective." Janot shakes his head. "We didn't make Seventy South, mates. The ice is too thick. Captain wants to see if Marco can fly to seventy from here on the ice shelf."

"Oh, boy." I start digging behind my bunk. "Some frogmen in Ushuaia hooked me up with a powered paraglider. I have no idea how to fly it. If you guys help me, we can launch from the ice." Ollie and Janot are not surprised. I scramble through my equipment stashed behind my fort. "Ollie, if you check the weather, I can have Janot and Abbo help me on the ice shelf."

Janot helps me move plastic cases and nylon dive bags around the tight quarters.

"Damn, we're so bloody close," Ollie mumbles as he storms topside to the pilot house.

"Winds are good out there, mate. It's bloody beautiful," says the French pirate.

"Thanks, Janot. This will be a major adventure if we pull this off."

"If we don't, we will bury you here with a proper cross and a sign."

"Yeah, what will it say?"

"Bien essaye," answers the Frenchman.

"Yeah? What does that mean?" I ask.

"I fucking tried."

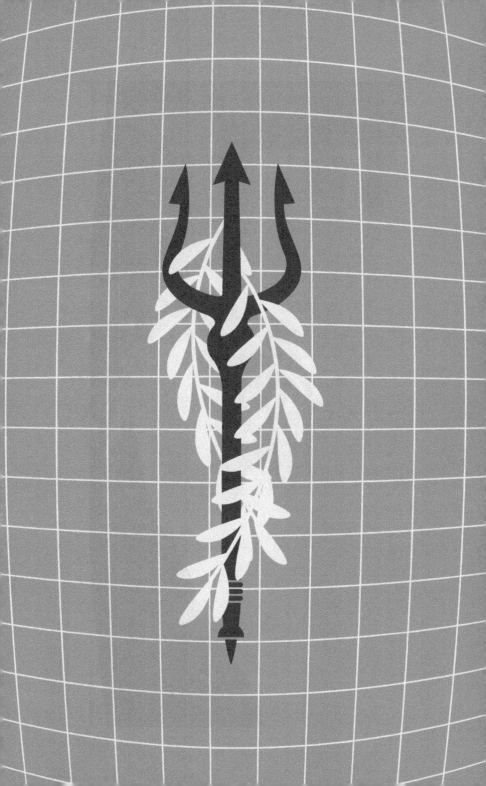

SEVENTY SOUTH

FLIGHT OF THE ALBATROSS

King George VI Ice Shelf
Antarctica *Seamaster* 69.5 degrees south latitude
FEBRUARY 2001
AUTHOR AGE: 34

Stepping out on the ice shelf of George VI is like landing a spaceship on a foreign planet. For the team, it is a surreal experience. The *Seamaster* has landed, and the captain has ordered the lunar rover to deploy. Each of us in the crew dons our "spacesuits," and I tuck away a few PowerBars near my body. My torso's heat will keep them warm and ready in case I have a long walk (or swim) back to the mothership.

I don the egg beater on my back, and Janot pull-starts the two stroke motor.

WAAAAaaaaAAAA

The motor comes alive. I situate the throttle on my left hand and squeeze the trigger.

The four-bladed wooden prop moves on my back and pushes me forward. It is an extremely unusual feeling!

With the egg beater spinning on my back in idle, I focus on inflating the parachute in the steady 9-knot breeze of the shelf. Abbo lays out the parachute and lines, as he has done for past flights for me.

45

As I am "kiting" the wing over my head, Janot makes final adjustments on the motor idle, avoiding the spinning prop inside a semi-protective cage.

The whole thing is quite a production, and simultaneously an adventure as we do a few test runs.

When I am kitted up, the two assisting crewmen step back, and I arc the wing over my head and spin around for a proper takeoff.

Takeoff? Hmmm. I never did this on a flat surface, what the hell do I do? I have only seconds with the wing over my head to gain forward speed or the whole thing collapses into a ball. On top of a spinning prop.

"Hit the fucking throttle, mate!!!" Janot yells from his safe place on the ice.

I give the contraption on my back full throttle, and the propeller roars to life, the unmuffled motor screaming into my ears.

The spinning blades pitch into a harmonious tone and an overwhelming force of wind pushes me forward.

What the hell do I do now?

"Fucking run, mate!"

I start running. However, something is not quite right.

The force of the prop on my back is pushing me down into the ice. My quadriceps are burning and flexing like the Incredible Hulk; only brute force is keeping me from being pushed face first into the ice. I pump my legs like wheels.

Janot and Abbo run along beside me down the endless runway.

"Leannn baaackkk, maaate!" says the French pirate, demonstrating running in a ridiculous aft-leaning posture.

I mimic the posture.

WOOOSHH!

My feet leave the ice, and I am airborne!

I climb in altitude, keeping the throttle hammered, and check my wrist altimeter. Five hundred feet. Roger that.

Check wing, check lines, good. I register everything in my brain.

The engine and prop roar behind my back.

Eight hundred feet. Roger that.

Nine hundred feet.

Below, the two yellow suits cheer me on.

Captain Blake is standing on the stern of *Seamaster* with a cup of tea and a satellite phone. Ollie is wearing a bathrobe and slippers standing next to him, a "cupper" in his hand as well. I know Sir Peter Blake is calling the UNEP conference in Europe. He chooses not to film this three-ring circus for the Discovery Channel show.

"Let me know when I can report Seventy South, Ollie," Sir Peter Blake says to his first mate who, at the moment, looks comically like Klinger from the TV show *M*A*S*H*.

High above the ice shelf, on the horizon, I spot a beautiful set of ice cliffs in front of me, the cliffs of Seventy South. I check my wrist altimeter.

One thousand feet.

Hooyah, one thousand feet!

BOOM!

I hit wind shear.

Down here, the wind shear is a pilot's worst nightmare, and that is with solid wings. For me, now possibly flying a paraglider farther south than anyone before, the brute force of the wind shear on the pillowcase I am using for a wing is devastating.

The result is a rapid spin back toward Earth and a partially collapsed parachute canopy.

React, Marcus Aurelius. Spread your risers apart and re-inflate the wing!

I watch the wing spin between myself and the ground in an arcing turn, and then feel my stomach in my mouth.

It is precisely like reaching the apex of the rollercoaster ride and taking the drop.

WHOAAA!

I have the good sense to release the death grip I have on the throttle and allow myself to fall below my canopy while staying upright, and not tumbling. The thought of my parachute lines tangled in the spinning prop is not good.

I have the flash of Janot hammering in the cross with the sign.

Bien essaye...

Not today, Frenchman.

Il a Conquis. I will conquer.

I pull outward on the webbing risers that attach my harness to my suspension lines. The wing catches air and inflates.

"Fuck!" I scream out loud, and only to myself.

I gather myself under canopy and check my brake lines. All is good.

I orient myself in direction and find the cliffs. I check my altimeter and register an altitude reading in the red. I am below five hundred feet. I hammer the throttle once more, and climb.

Below on the shelf is a mother Weddell seal and her pups staring up at me, thoroughly enjoying the show.

Beyond the family is a solitary penguin lying on its back, apparently having a heart attack watching this giant bird of prey swooping in on it.

This will definitely not make the TV show, I promise myself.

Not long after takeoff, I return to Earth and proudly report to Ollie.

"Seventy South, mate."

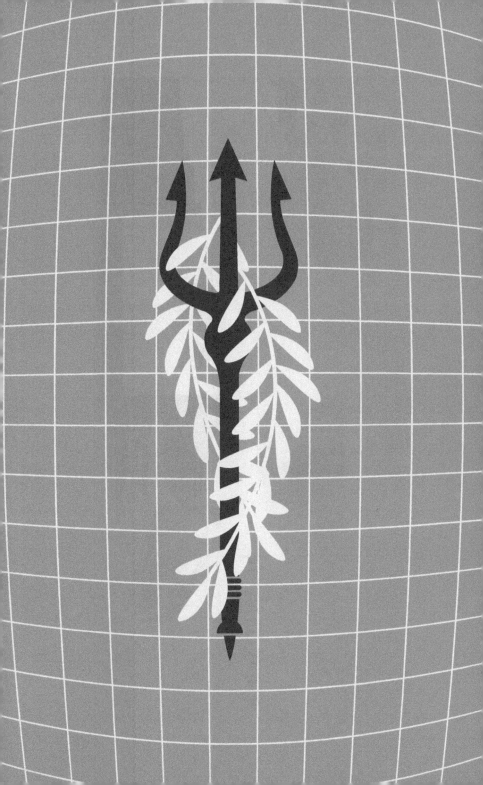

Seventy South

BEAST UNDER THE ICE

Author's note: This chapter is dedicated to the memory
of one of the research divers at the last station that
Blakexpeditions visited on our journey south.

*Kirsty Brown of the British Antarctic Survey was tragically
killed two years later by a leopard seal in 2003 off the shore of
Rothera Base. She was snorkeling and captured in the jaws of
an eleven-foot leopard and dragged to a depth of 200 feet and
drowned as the seal reportedly had her entire head in its mouth.*

Seventy South Latitude
YEAR: SPRING 2001
AUTHOR AGE: 34

Diving under the ice at Seventy South was, for me, the high point
of the Antarctic Expedition. As a dive crew, Janot, Ollie, the
Discovery Channel cameraman, and I are as tight as it gets. We
have the best dry suits to keep us warm, and full face masks with
radios to protect areas not covered by a dive hood. Sir Peter Blake
opts out of the cold-water dives and remains topside monitoring
our radio communications. He always has warm scones waiting
for the four of us when we return to warmer temperatures inside
Seamaster's belly.

The three of us dive daily for more than two weeks, capturing
rare footage of the undersea world around us, finding our most
rewarding experiences with the whales and the seals.

Diving under the ice with the whales represents "the holy grail of diving" for me. After all of my time underwater as a SEAL, this is a reward.

The dive team and I fix ourselves below the ice shelf and film humpback and Minke whales as they surface in the clear blue of the open water, take a deep breath, and swim under the shelf to join us in the shadows.

The whales would swim into the black curtain under the ice shelf and navigate along the cracks and fissures of the glowing ceiling as if entering a sacred church with stained-glass windows.

The repeated visions of the giant cetaceans sharing such tight quarters under the glowing beams of the ceiling often brought goosebumps to my skin. It is as if I am watching life on another planet, or dimension, beyond life here on Earth.

Above the surface, the humpbacks would sing us to sleep through the hull of *Seamaster*.

As divers, our second favorite encounters under the ice were with the furry baby seals that would visit us and swim by our side. Always curious and friendly, they were an amazing wonderment to me, especially the younger ones.

All of us took a liking to the pups. One young female in particular would watch the team from the safety of the surface and then dive under the ice shelf to join us as we made our way deep into its recesses.

Our team would pierce the black wall of the ice shelf's shadow to enter an entirely new world in a spectrum of light. The cracks in the ice ceiling are like light beams illuminating this secret world, and the three seal pups come down to join us as I and Janot begin to screw in their ice anchors.

The female seal pup makes a game of blowing bubbles into each of our masked faces.

Ollie and the cameraman look like tiny specks due to the water's clarity and their distance from me and Janot.

The two are setting up for a shot of the Minke whales diving into the dark space under the ice. They will film them swimming in the glowing light under the shelf and feel the force of the water from their flukes from the moving hydraulics of such massive creatures.

Seeing the young pinniped now swimming below my feet, I catch the outer space-like immensity of where I am. The ocean's floor is more than 3,000 feet below me.

As the seal pup plays beneath me, I shift my ballast. I purge all the air from my dry suit and direct my head straight down to the depths of the Southern Ocean.

I hit my buoyancy compensator and puff some air into it with a button on my vest and the bottom of my feet and dive fins push upward to the icy roof above me.

Completely inverted, I stare down into the abyss. I feel I am completing a key moment in my journey. The light rays are piercing the cathedral roof, now at my feet, and plunging below me as far as my eyes can see.

The young seal is moving in the shafts of light below me, looking like an aquatic angel. I can only hear the sound of my breathing and my bubbles. I find a calm spot between my bubbles and the burden of my equipment, and I meditate.

For a moment, I am completely at peace. There always seems to be one spoiler in all my adventures.

Down in the Antarctic, it is the leopard seal.

If I had my choice to deal with a great white shark or a leopard seal, I would go with the shark.

In our experiences with the leopards much farther north, we collectively learned they are amazingly territorial and unrelenting in curiosity. Combined with a level of unpredictability and a massive set of jaws and body mass—they are over twelve feet long—the intimidation factor is high.

To give an idea of scale, I would equate the width of the leopard seal's jaws to the width of a muscular man's shoulders. When something that large is only inches from your dive mask, or sneaking up behind you in dark, murky water and holding its position there for minutes on end, it is extremely intimidating, to say the least.

The head is different from the average friendly looking seal; it is shaped like a serpent's head.

Farther north, the curious leopard seal eats penguin with reckless abandon. Its large jaws and teeth capture the aquatic birds both under the surface and sometimes right off the edge of the ice. It first punctures a penguin's skin in a half-moon-shaped bite; it bites the penguin over the head and whips the body violently from side to side, literally peeling off the skin. Sometimes it will play with the penguin in various states of disassembly. It is just downright mean.

I have no love for the leopard seal. We learned about them at the closest research station in Rothera, hundreds of miles north of us, when a research scientist took us under her protective wings and taught us the ropes with the leopards.

Rule number one is simply get out of the water when one is present. She told us that the food supply is dwindling below 65 degrees latitude, and her scientists had rumors of the leopards feeding on seals instead of penguins.

The thought of being tossed and skinned is not a good picture to dive with, let alone being caught in their jaws and dragged down into the depths to be drowned and then eaten.

The other thing she taught us is that leopards down here are known to pin themselves up to the roof of the ice and let out the most curious moans. The sound can best be described as creepy.

There were a few times under the ice that we heard the moans, but we didn't know what they were coming from at the time.

In our initial dives here at Seventy South, we witnessed a seal being killed by a large leopard seal and it left a lasting impression on us. Down here, we do not look much different from the seals. The leopards up north are curious, almost playful, and territorial. Down here it's a different story. This is much more dangerous. Janot approaches me and gives me a signal that something is wrong. I level off in flight and follow him to the clear blue edge of the shelf. Ollie and the cameraman come up behind us.

The seal pup bolts in front of us from side to side and we see the giant leopard seal for the first time.

The beast is massive!

At least twelve feet long, its serpent-like head is the size of a fifty-gallon fuel drum. Its large teeth are bared and attempting to capture the young Weddell rushing past us.

A nearby mother Weddell lures the beast away. The young seal pup takes the opportunity and launches her body from under the water, popping herself up onto the ice-shelf above us.

Janot and I watch the shape move above us through the blue and white ice.

WHOOOSHHHH!

The leopard swims like a rocket and launches its huge body onto the ice above us, its huge, dark shadow slithering like a snake in pursuit of the seals on the surface.

It is a horrifying sight.

"What iz thiz shit?" Janot says over the radio.

"We make a break for it and swim for Seamaster *lads,"* Ollie replies.

"It's too far, Ollie!" I exclaim.

"Let's go for the ice, mates," Janot insists.

"No fucking way, mate," I argue. "We'll get stuck trying to get over the edge and dragged down."

"Right then, we wait," reasons Ollie.

It is our only choice.

The leopard returns to the water shortly after our conversation, fortunately without a seal in its jaws. Unfortunately, it is not distracted by anything now but us.

We are stuck.

The leopard charges back and forth at the edge of the ice, taunting us to come out into the open depths of blue. We hold our position.

The beast bolts down into the depths and enters the shadows under our dive fins, at least fifty feet below.

"*Oh, sheet!*" says Janot.

"*We have to move,*" Ollie urges.

He grabs the cameraman and swims out into the blue. Janot hits me on the back of my dive hood and I swat at his hand to keep him clear of my head. I feel dense rubber against my swatting glove, not a human.

I turn around to the face of the leopard seal poking me with its nose. My response is a huge cloud of bubbles from my regulator. The leopard responds to my actions in characteristic form.

One thing we learned while diving with leopards up north is that they consider blowing bubbles a sign of aggression. My biological needs and involuntary actions at the moment do not please the beast.

It gets right in my face and blows bubbles back at me. The leopard seal has gotten so close to me that it completely crowds me up against the ice above and its body below. I cannot even kick my feet.

I could easily panic at this moment. I do not.

I remember my experience tying five knots in BUD/S, about being calm under water, conserving air, relaxing my muscles. I look into the serpent's dark eyes and I remember the lesson.

Play dead, I think. *Don't bolt off!*

I wait for the beast to back off of me—it does not.

The four of us have one hundred yards of open water to navigate to the stern ladder of *Seamaster*. It is too far to bolt.

The leopard stays on top of me and crowds my space, forcing its massive head back into my regulator. I worry it is going to snap at my mask and rip it from my face, if not take my entire head in its jaws. Either option is going to suck.

I cannot get away from the beast. Janot grabs me from behind and drags me out of the shadows, putting space between me and the beast.

He pulls me into the group, and Ollie comes over my shoulder and pushes us farther off the leopard. It is an incredibly brave move.

Our group huddles together to move away from the seal. For a long while it stays in place, then finally, it swims off.

We have been clearing our ears in irritation, but not paying attention to our bodies and our equipment, everything here is uncomfortable. Janot points to his dive computer and throws it in my face. He has 200 psi left in his tank, bare bones. We have only minutes of air. He uses as much as me on a good day, so I know I am low as well.

But what he is calling attention to is our depth.

As a team, we are stuck in a downdraft of water. What used to be twenty feet of depth has turned into one hundred feet!

Suddenly I look up at a speck of Seamaster instead of over to it.

"Keeck your fins!" Janot says to all of us over our intercoms.

Ollie catches on and the three of us kick up.

The cameraman is starting to lose it. He is focused on the large underwater camera housing in his hands and continues to sink.

He becomes a tiny speck in the clear water.

I check my dive computer…400psi. "I'll get him, Janot. You stay with Ollie."

I kick down with my most efficient dolphin kick and move smooth and fast, conserving as much air as possible.

I make it to the Discovery film guy and grab the camera housing from his hands. I signal him to kick up and notice the glazed look in his eyes. I put two puffs of air in his BC and level him off.

I grab him and kick to the surface. The air expanding in his vest, he begins to rise with me.

"Kick!" I yell into my radio.

He gets it, and we make it to Ollie and Janot.

We turn back to *Seamaster* and begin the swim back, and the leopard returns. This time I use the camera housing to keep away from its aggressive jaws.

The four of us swim to the boat while I use the lens of the camera housing as a spacer, and the beast repeatedly lunges at me. I pivot myself to its lunge and the group of divers moves behind me as one body.

Together as a team, we conquered this beast.

If we had panicked and split up as single units we would have gotten picked off one by one, and we would have lost a cameraman to the abyss.

Definitely a bonding moment for us as more than an expedition team. As a family. When we make it to *Seamaster*, Alistair and Sir Peter have the Zodiac in the water with the motor running.

Alistair is coxswain and Sir Peter is up on the bow with a large pole that we use to push ice away from the hull of the vessel.

Abbo guns the motor toward us while Sir Peter hefts the long silver pole above his head and gives the leopard seal a whack right on its head.

Sir Peter looks like Captain Ahab himself from the fabled *Moby Dick* as he fends the beast back from his ship. We quickly mount the ladder one by one and exit the water.

I am the last one still floating with the camera housing as Abbo drives the boat up to me. The captain has a big smile under his big bushy mustache.

"Welcome back, Mr. Lonergan. Hot scones and tea await you in the galley, mate."

I can only nod and give him a wink through my dive mask. With the end of our most eventful dive yet, it is time for us to head north before we are trapped in the growing ice.

Winter is surrounding us on all sides.

AVOIDING SHACKLETON

Southern Ocean
Seamaster **latitude 69.5 South**
MARCH 2001
AUTHOR AGE: 34

With a stack of legal paperwork in his hands, the captain gives the entire crew, including the Discovery Channel folks, a stern warning over breakfast.

"I have to have each of you sign this waiver. It states you understand we may be trapped in the ice, like Shackleton, and you each understand we may have to live aboard the vessel until the next thaw." He passes out the documents.

"Sign on the dotted line. And Mr. Lonergan, use your legal name please," he says with a shit-eating grin. "Ollie, make preparations to get us underway. There is a storm coming and we have a short window to make it out of here and back to the safety Trinity Island. From there we have a straight shot back to Ushuaia."

"Aye!" says the First Mate.

"You men heard the captain. Let's stow the gear. Janot, fire up the engines and get her warm. Abbo, climb to the crow's nest and find us a path out of the icebergs. Marco, retrieve the bowline from the ice."

"Aye, Ollie," I respond. The others simply get to work.

Sir Peter pulls me aside. "Oh, and Mr. Lonergan, good job under the ice, mate. That footage will make the TV show for Discovery."

"Thanks, Pete," I say proudly, then shuffle into my yellow survival suit.

"I'm going to be counting on you up on the bow in the coming nights. We can hit these bergy-bits in the calm water, and we can push them around, but the hull cannot take the impact of the icebergs in rough water, you understand?"

"Yes, Capitan," I respond. I try to appear calm, but my heart is about to jump out of my chest and hide back under the ice shelf with the leopard seal.

Gulp.

The journey out of Seventy South starts with a bang.

Abbo stays up in the crow's nest as we bounce off of what seems like a growing field of icebergs. It's as if we are finding ourselves in a giant slushy as ice seems to come out of nowhere and coagulate into the King George VI Sound.

I stand bow watch for the first leg of our journey, helping the captain navigate through pieces of ice that start as the size of the kitchen sink. No problemo. Next they grow to the size of a car.

By the time the evening stars start to shine, which we hadn't seen for a while now, the ice chunks are as big as Mack trucks.

Moments earlier I had my feet up on the guard rails that surround the bulbous nose of our ice breaker class sailing vessel.

The rail is supposed to keep us from going over the bow in instances exactly like this. The designer built Seamaster to explore the poles, so a great deal of thought went into her design. The anchor sits in a hold about twelve inches below my feet. The rail comes in handy when we are doing anchoring operations as well, especially in rough seas.

Being a sheep of a different color, and contemplating the possible uses for this rail, I always find a way to use things differently to help me achieve my mission. Sometimes for the better, but often-times I fail.

For my job as bow watch since we left Ushuaia, I prefer to be elevated high above the deck to get a better view, and keep my feet a little drier.

I climb onto the rails and use them as a perch, similar to a hawk on a tree branch. To maintain my balance, I lean back on a large metal cable that runs from the bow up to the main mast. It is an important cable to keep the mast from pulling back toward the stern. It also serves as a guide for our foresail when we deploy it. It is a rather precarious perch.

In this case, we are not sailing, we are motoring.

Pete has our keel run up as shallow as possible to avoid hitting ice, so our bottom is smooth, the props guarded in large metal cages that will support the weight of the vessel if we end up on top of the ice.

Today, in the large ice flow, I have the good judgement to jump down to the deck and brace myself on the protective railing of the bow.

It is a good move.

Abbo comes over his Marine band walkie-talkie and exclaims something that gives us all goose bumps.

"Captain, we're closed in. No way out!"

Sir Peter comes up on the radio from the pilot house. "Fuck that, there is always a way out, mate. Find us one!"

"Aye, there's some thin layers of ice off the starboard beam, we may be able to break through there!"

"Roger, mate. All hands on deck! Brace yourselves for impact!"

Sir Peter runs the engines to full throttle and runs Seamaster right up onto a large ice flow blocking us from a tiny rivulet of open water that will take us farther north. It is a bold and brave move by the great sea captain. He does not hesitate, he commits.

BOOOOOMMMM!!!!

The hull of *Seamaster* shudders from the impact of the ice. The entire vessel shakes in a violent spasm as it adjusts from the liquid to the solid state under her hull. She takes the shot like a heavyweight prizefighter and powers on.

Sir Peter rams the throttle full speed as the ship comes to a resting halt on the ice. We are at a dead stop, with half of the vessel out of the water and on top of the large sheet of ice.

There is a pregnant pause in the drama as everything comes to a silent halt. Pete backs off the props when they begin to come out of the water.

Oh shit.

Abbo comes over the radio. *"The ice is cracking, Pete!"*

Sir Peter responds on the ship's intercom. *"All hands up on the bow!!!"*

It is a totally futile effort, but we all do our part.

Ollie comes up carrying a bag of dive weights in a large bag, and the film crew runs up with Janot carrying God knows what from the engine room. I jump up and down on the bow. It is a comical scene indeed.

Nothing happens.

Then: *WHHHOOOOOSSSHHHHH!!!*

The ice breaks under the hull of our beautiful icebreaker and we settle into the liquid world once again. It is a delicious feeling to bob once again.

All of us on the bow shout for joy. Sir Peter doesn't have time to celebrate. He slams the throttle and powers us into a narrow channel of seawater.

"Abbo, find us a fucking path out of here. Marco, get back on watch. Janot, check the engines, we ran the props out of the water. Ollie, get up here, I need a piss, mate!"

And so it goes for two days and two nights, until the fateful evening I get washed overboard.

It is all a harrowing experience, and one none of us will ever forget.

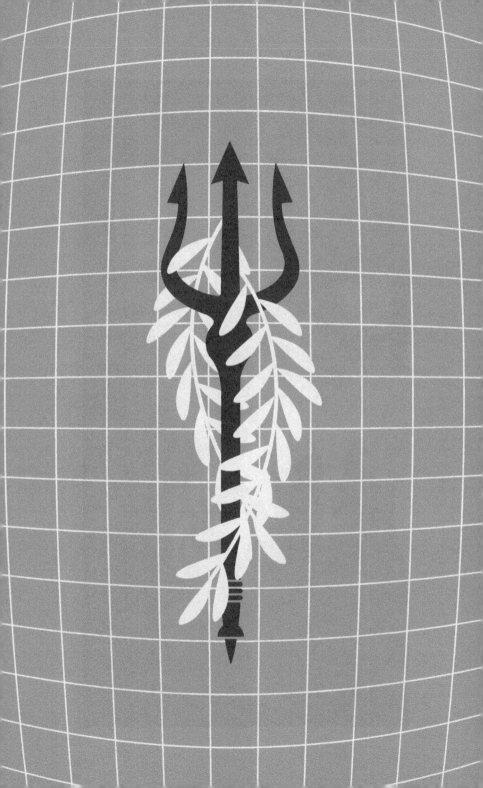

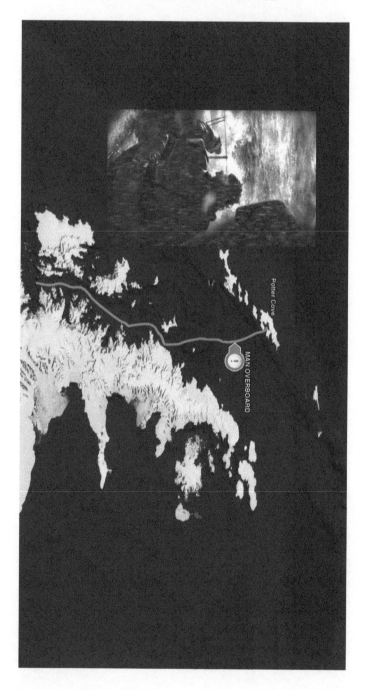

MAN OVERBOARD: PART II

I was scanning furiously for icebergs.
It was my turn on bow watch on a night that I will never
forget. I was knocked off my watch station, hanging by my
rescue tether. The men of Blakexpeditions saved my life.
Gratefully we make it to the safety of Potter Cove.

LOCATION: Potter Cove, South Shetland Islands
DATE: 10 March 2001
TIME-0845 HRS
AUTHOR AGE: 34

I wake up on an island in the South Shetlands after an exhausting night at sea, our final night in the ice fields of Antarctica.

I pushed myself too hard trying to handle everything up front on my own last night. My mistake almost cost us our lives. I am lucky to have such a great team. We are all survivors. I still feel stiff in the neck from Ollie grabbing me and pulling me back on to the deck of Seamaster last night.

It is an awesome kind of sore.

I rub my eyes and wonder if I am still alive, or maybe in Heaven. A curious penguin is staring at me and extending a flipper, almost greeting me to the island.

I think that if I am dead, then God certainly does have a great sense of humor. I mean, who better to meet me at the pearly gates after hitting an iceberg in the middle of the night in Antarctica than a friendly penguin?

Bien essaye!

I come to my senses when I smell the stink of a penguin rookery.

I look out to the vessel anchored offshore in the calm waters of the cove. Sir Peter Blake is writing in the captain's log while the evening is still fresh on his mind.

First, we escaped the ice with some outstanding pilotage and a lot of luck. Second, Seamaster had a visit from a great white albatross that Sir Peter desperately wanted to see on this adventure south. The giant bird had eluded him for the entire expedition.

In his captain's log, Sir Peter Blake had this to say about the storm that evening:

Sir Peter Blake's Ship's Log Entry

ANTARCTICA - DTG: 10 March 2001
Lat/Long: 62.14 South / 58.42 West
Description: Potter Cove, South Shetland Islands
Weather: Wind 40 knots / Driving Sleet and Snow
Air Temp: -2 degrees C
Sea Temp: 0 degrees C
Visibility: Very Poor

1800 hours. We left Trinity Island yesterday, headed for Discovery Bay on Greenwich Island. As evening approached, a large pack of brash ice, sea ice, and icebergs appeared ahead and blocked our path.

There were only four hours of daylight and 35 miles to go. We decided to press on, hoping to reach Discovery in time for dinner, even though we were heading 90 degrees from our intended course.

We headed northwest for three hours to try and get around the ice, but there was no way through.

The patch extended as far as the eye could see from the deck and it was too rough to send someone up to the crow's nest on the mast.

The wind rose as the evening progressed until it was in the 35-40 knot range, driving before it a fine sleet that covered everything. There was so much ice in the water that we were continually having to take avoiding action. Clothing on deck was full cold weather gear. Spray from the bow was turning to ice crystals as it blew over the boat.

The winches and most of the ropes were frozen stiff, and with ice shards falling from the sails and rigs, it was important to be wearing goggles to protect you from getting the shards in the face.

Gradually the decks became sheets of ice, the seawater now froze on the lifelines as it left the now steep waves as heavy spray, and forward visibility was reduced to 100 meters or so.

So there we were, trying to find a way through floating ice of all sizes, in a gale, with driving sleet in the middle of the night.

We kept a crew of two on the bow with a searchlight looking for bergs. Marco, Abbo, Janot, and Ollie shared this role.

They were harnessed on in full survival suits and regularly covered with spray from the bow going under.

At times the flows pinched in on both sides so that we had to slow down and squeeze through the narrowest of gaps, not exactly sure how we were going to make it until the last moment.

By midnight we had entered Potter Cove using only radar. That evening we used the big diesel heater in the salon to keep the insides warm and cozy as the outside conditions turned to near zero visibility.

I have raced through the Southern Ocean a number of times and had near misses with ice and seen many bergs, but I have never had a night like the one we have just experienced. It will certainly be recalled as one of the high points in our journey, but one that I will be pleased to not repeat too often.

—*Sir Peter Blake*

Janot and I collect ourselves from our nap on the beach. The Frenchman was awakened by one of the birds shooting a jet of poop on to him like a water pistol.

"You sheet on me you little bird? I sheet on you!"

I can only laugh my guts out while I watch him chase the waddling penguins around the shoreline.

It is indeed great to be alive.

When we return to *Seamaster*, I sit down with Sir Peter over some large maps of the Amazon Basin.

He gives me the assignment to fly north to Brazil and scout a three thousand-mile journey for us to document the Amazon jungle as part of our expedition program. This segment will ultimately be filmed for the National Geographic Channel.

No pressure.

Sir Peter tells me that the film crew found Jacques-Yves Cousteau's original guide for his Amazon expedition in the 1980s.

The guide's name is Miguel da Silva.

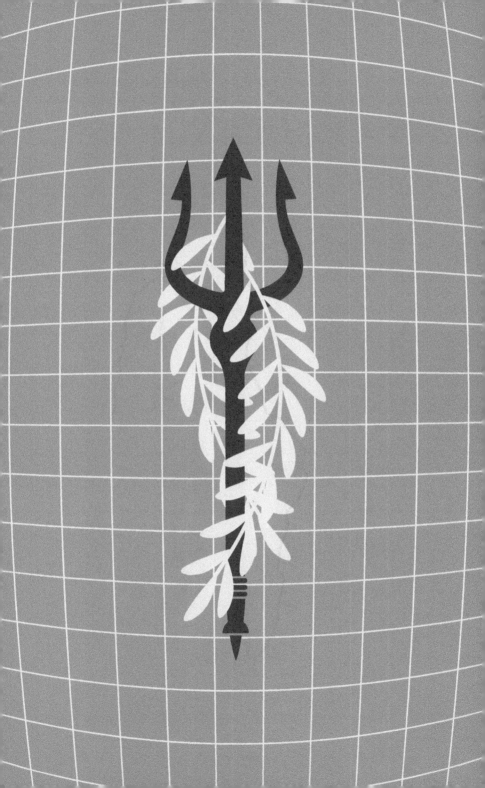

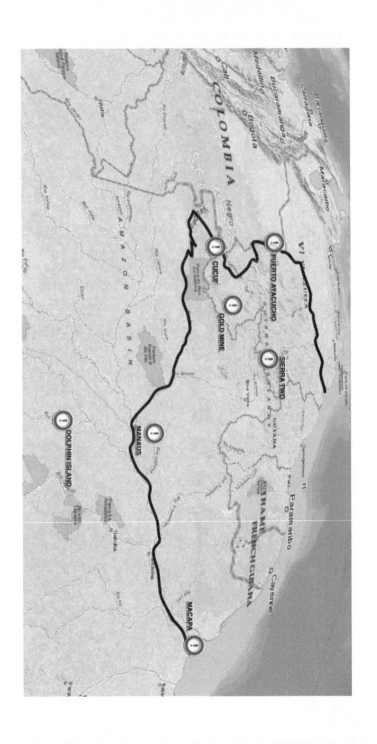

THE AMAZON

The Vessel *Iguana*
River of Doubt, Brazil
SPRING 2001
AUTHOR AGE: 34

Miguel da Silva is a gentleman and a true explorer in every sense of the word.

Miguel is in his early 60s, and was Jacques-Yves Cousteau's guide during the famous captain's expeditions to the Amazon in the 1980s. Miguel is my guide today.

My friend has made it his responsibility to help me plan a 1,500-mile journey from the mouth of the Rio Amazonas at the Atlantic, midway across the continent to the city of Manaus, and up the Rio Negro to the Venezuelan border.

In short, he is helping me plan the Blakexpeditions journey I discussed with Sir Peter Blake in Antarctica.

I am lying in my bunk aboard the river vessel *Iguana*. This is the same riverboat utilized by Jacques Cousteau to do the same type of scouting before he brought in his team of explorers.

I am in good company today, with Miguel mastering the vessel and itinerary, One-Eyed Jack at the helm (literally one eye), and Paulo the flamboyant cook down in the galley working away on the evening meal of fish he caught at an earlier stop along the flowing river.

As I sit for my meal with the captain I observe the well-appointed table located on the aft fantail of the riverboat.

The table is set for three, with a white linen table cloth and fine china and silverware. It is a large rectangular table, with place settings for twelve. Miguel had recently completed a hosted expedition for some Japanese researchers up into the reaches of the Rio Negro to the north. It was a big group.

He turned away all his business to focus solely on me for the planning portions of this journey.

This makes for a peaceful experience with such a serene man.

Miguel sits on the side corner of the table in a white cotton button-down shirt. His sleeves are long, and they are rolled up to his elbows. This is a good sign, as this means the bugs are not out yet.

I am wearing my Columbia PFG expedition shirt. It is a lightweight, vented button-down shirt with long sleeves and covered mesh on my back to breathe. It is the same type of shirt as those designed for fly fishermen. I love this shirt.

I am wearing long pants as well. They are olive drab green poplin military pants, the same ones the soldiers wore in Vietnam. I have several pairs that I bought in an Army surplus store back in the States. I have green paracord at the base of the legs to close them up around my ankles to prevent creepy crawlies from making their way up my legs.

No one on the riverboat wears shoes until we have to go ashore. It is then I don a pair of rubber-soled canvas Israeli desert boots. They are perfect for the jungle, as they are always wet. The canvas helps them dry quickly in the hot Brazilian sun and the soft rubber soles wrap around slippery branches and cling to mud with their deep treads.

My feet are tan from my time on the boat. If I am not in my room, I am on the roof the pilot house with my feet dangling over the edge and in front of One-Eyed Jack. He doesn't mind since I usually sit on his blind side. He is always scanning the river for changes in the shifting banks and islands of the quick flowing river that vacillates in width from several miles to several feet of navigable space.

Miguel offers me the head of the table, as he always does, holding his hand out to guide me into my chair. He reminds me of a happy Buddha in his jovial appearance and movements. His eyes and his smile remind me of the Dalai Lama.

Miguel has a mop of hair on his head with straight black hairs peppered with gray, showing his 60 odd years. He does not have the dark skin of the traditional Brazilian man. He is lightskinned and avoids long exposure to the sun. He looks more Portuguese than Brazilian.

Next to Miguel is a young Brazilian woman. She is about twenty years old and professional in appearance and dress. Her name is Katia, and she is Miguel's personal assistant and primary administrator of all his expedition affairs.

Katia looks like the character Pocahontas from the Walt Disney animation. Her tan face is perfectly framed by her jet black hair. Shuffling through papers on her side of the table, she does not look up at me.

"Marco, welcome to your lunch!" It is Paulo the ship's chef announcing himself from the ship's galley in his typically flamboyant style.

Paulo reminds me of the character Agador in the Robin Williams movie *The Birdcage*. Paulo wears the same cut-off jean shorts, a cut-off belly shirt, and bare feet.

"Hi, Paulo. Thank you for cooking for us today."

"Oh, Marco, I hope you enjoy your meat service. It is a pleasure to prepare."

"Thanks all the same."

"Paulo, you have everything for drinks you need?" Miguel asks with a wry smile. He enjoys watching people having a good time bantering back and forth.

"Caipirinhas!" Paulo shouts, running back to the galley to fetch the food and drinks.

"You handle him well, Marco. Most guests don't know what to make of him."

"Yeah, well I know he is up to mischief any time he shows up without food or drinks in his hands."

"You got that right." Miguel pulls out a large paper map and spreads it out on the empty part of the table. "Let's discuss this expedition." He places a finger on the map. "We are here. This is the first one hundred miles tracing Roosevelt's journey backward from Manaus. His journey was a total of one thousand miles that began near the Bolivian border to the west. He made his way to our current location, then paddled upriver to the headwaters to our south.

"This will be your choice: One thousand miles to the south of Manaus to retrace Roosevelt to the River of Doubt, or one thousand miles to the west of Manaus to retrace JYC's expedition to the River of Gold."

"An awesome comparison, Miguel," I say. "I love the choice. What's west?"

"Cousteau split up his team, Marco," he explains. "He navigated Calypso up the Amazonas to the Peruvian border of Iquitos far to the west." Miguel moves his pointer along the map. "He sent his son, Jean-Michel, up into the Andes, where he climbed and descended the origins of the Amazon River through its whitewater rapids with a makeshift raft."

"No kidding, Miguel; I love it!"

"I will tell you a secret. I spent significant time with the captain. He had his helicopter and a float plane. I took him on a journey by air up north to the Rio Negro and into the tepuis of Venezuela. He wanted to return for that; to him this was his favorite place. He did not care for the river west."

"Wow, Miguel. What's at the end of our journey to the south following Teddy Roosevelt? They say this journey up what is now called Roosevelt River is a cursed journey."

"My answer, Mr. Marcus, is danger, disease, and death to the south." Miguel sips his coffee and stares deep into his steaming mug.

"Not encouraging, my friend."

"They say the River of Doubt was the death of a great leader, warrior, and explorer. They say his journey down the River of Doubt killed him, as he died from infections shortly after returning to the States."

Miguel looks out to the jungle as the *Iguana* chugs against the flowing current from the highlands.

"If it is an adventure you seek, Mr. Marcus, then the journey south is your answer."

"There would have to be considerable benefits to compete with those risks, Miguel."

"Indeed. To the south lies treasure, prehistoric tribes, pirates, and beautiful women."

"I'm in, Miguel. This will be the perfect route."

"Not so fast, Mr. Marcus."

"What?"

"I mentioned the danger," he says with a coy grin.

"I am thinking you drop me off down here for a couple of months and I figure things out." Miguel chuckles at the absurdity of the statement and stops mid-giggle when he realizes I am serious.

"Miguel, what lies at the end of the River of Doubt? Why did he make the trek?"

"Roosevelt heard of the unexplored Plains of Pareces. The flat top mountains are an amazingly beautiful oasis above the endless canopy of the Amazon that serves as the headwaters. The isolated area is close to the Peruvian/Bolivian border. The area is rich in diamonds and guarded by the Lost Tribes."

"I know about the tribes. I trained the Peruvian version of their SEAL snipers; it's cowboy country down there."

"Yes, when Roosevelt made his expedition it was the early nineteen hundreds. They were followed along the entire journey by a pack of indigenous warriors of Cinta Larga."

"I'm familiar with them…they don't mess around. The warriors are named after the large belts on their waists to hold their meat carving knives. Even the local soldiers call them 'The Hunters of Men.'"

"Today they guard one of the world's largest diamond mines in the region. They recently killed some settlers trying to clear cut on their dedicated land."

"Wow, Miguel. Do you think we could meet them through the FUNAI connections you have?"

"I could try, Marcus."

"Like I said earlier, Miguel, cowboy country." I shift my thoughts. "You mentioned the women. What's up with that?"

"Yes, this is the region of Amazonas many of the dancers you see in Carnival come from. Beautiful and amazing dancers indeed." Miguel points to Katia, cradling her cherublike face in his hands. "Katia is from this place. She is from the closest settlement to our south, Via do Carmo."

"Now I know why Teddy Roosevelt wanted to go up the river and into the highlands…treasure, women, wild nature, and dangerous Indians. I'm definitely interested!"

"I can drop you off on an island upriver for a few days while I head into town." On his paper chart of the Roosevelt River Miguel indicates a small island up the river with a large sandy beach and a tuft of trees for shelter.

"I will leave Katia with you. It is best she does not show her face in this city, there are many that want her to return, even against her will." Miguel puts a comforting hand on his assistant's shoulder. "It will take me two days to reach Via do Carmo, about one hundred miles." Miguel traces the route south with his weathered finger. "Plan on one week. We can leave you some supplies."

"Thanks, Miguel. Can you lend me one of your maps?"

"No problem. You can keep this one."

Miguel hands me his precious map. The parchment is soft and well folded but well taken care of, despite the environment.

I will use this as my only map for the remainder of the year. It is the same one he used with Jacques Cousteau and covers the entire Amazon Basin. This map will save my life.

"Would you like me to drop Paulo off with you as well?" Miguel asks me with a grin.

"No, Miguel, thanks all the same."

"Just kidding. You don't think I am going to lend you my favorite cook, do you?"

"Keep him. Katia and I will be fine. Just leave us with some coffee and that coffee pot."

"You will get more than that, my friend."

Dolphin Island

Cucui

Ayacucho

Aracamoni

Sierra Two

MANAUS, BRAZIL

Macapa

DOLPHIN ISLAND

River of Doubt—Amazon Basin
SPRING 2001
AUTHOR AGE: 34

I wade across a lagoon of warm fresh water with Katia by my side. The water is crystal clear but tinged with pulses of muddy water that flow downstream from the mountainous region of the Pareces.

Katia is wearing a soft, loose-fitting white cotton shirt. The buttons are each made of shells from the river. She wears no bra, as I find most women in the region prefer. Her lower half is partially covered by a wraparound sarong with a pink Roxy surfing bikini underneath.

The white sand of the river bottom here makes more for a tropical setting than the dense, bug infested jungle scene I would expect. Although I am covered, Katia appears inoculated from any inconvenience from bugs.

For me, this is not a hardship at all. This is straight out of the movie *Blue Lagoon,* but this is as far as that fantasy goes. I'm here to plan an expedition, not hit on women. I keep it respectful with my travel mate, as I learned from years past as a mountain guide. Yet there is something else.

I recognize a quiet reserve I have deep inside, not allowing myself to get too close to someone, to give me space in case something bad happens to them—or me.

It hits me hard on Dolphin Island with Katia, and I will never forget it. It's the primary reason I am neither married nor have children yet. For some reason, I make adventure the primary driver in my decision-making process.

Katia holds a large bladed knife in her hand as if it is a part of her body, and has a leather bag draped over her right shoulder that contains various items, including some gathered nuts and a few pieces of fruit.

I take inventory of our supplies.

First, my trusty machete. The flimsy piece of steel in my hand was a leaf spring from an old Jeep that someone sharpened along one edge and into a rounded tip. The wooden handle is well-worn and made of a hard, polished wood, but it has a good grip even when it's wet, which is more often than not.

I am wearing a wide brim floppy hat to shade myself from the intense sun down here, almost directly on the equator. My button-down lightweight fly fishing shirt is secured to my neck and the sleeves are rolled down and secure at each wrist. There are no bugs, yet.

I am wearing my Vietnam-era military style poplin combat trousers and tie the laces that secure the pant legs around my ankles. In my waterproof backpack, I have two pairs of wool socks and a pair of surfing shorts, my Israeli desert boots, and a pair of Teva sandals. These are the only clothes I will wear for the next six months. I have no need for any other clothing out here as long as I take good care of what I have.

This island is my first challenge away from Miguel for more than a few hours. I know it is a test. He is trusting me with the care of Katia, or perhaps it is the other way around.

This area is relatively safe compared to the options ahead. Miguel will learn how I handle myself before he takes me any further than this island. This I know through instinct, this is real explorer stuff.

In my backpack is a filter for my drinking water, and a nylon pouch that holds my medical kit.

Doc Fullerton hooked me up with a proper SEAL jungle pack of supplies I used on my regular forays with him and my sniper partner, Phap. I know every item in the kit and where it is. I know every drug and how to use it. My most precious medical item is my crazy glue. I do not have suture equipment in my kit, only glue.

Miguel left us with a cooking pot, a coffee pot, and a frying pan. I have a box of waterproof matches, a basket of fruit, and some vegetables.

As I learned from my Force Recon days, I always traveled with a bag of instant rice in my backpack, a spare lighter, and a Leatherman tool. I have a waterproof headlamp with spare batteries, a large roll of parachute cord, and some duct tape.

Miguel has stocked us up with extra rice, a bottle of whiskey, and a live chicken that Paulo carried ashore wearing nothing but a pair of cut-off shorts and a smile.

Katia has the chicken tied up to a large, shady tree near the forest and is starting to organize what we have left.

Paulo also hands me a fishing pole with tackle off of *Iguana*, and One-Eyed Jack paddles a dugout kayak to the beach and hauls it to a safe perch above the water.

"Marcus, take this radio," Miguel calls to me from the bow of the riverboat anchored in the soft sand of the river bank.

I wade out to him along the starboard flank of the boat so he does not have to throw the radio down to me.

He walks to the side and hands me a large walkie-talkie. "This is VHF and I am on channel 16."

"Got it, Miguel. Give me a call as soon as you are heading back and we will prepare a meal for you and Paulo."

"Good, Marcus. Plan on three. I may have a guest when I return."

"Very good, Capitan. Dinner for five on the island."

"You need to name this island my friend," he says. "It has no name."

"I have a week to figure it out!"

"Let us hope not more than that. Remember, life is unpredictable down here."

"That is why I have dependable friends, Miguel. Nothing but the best. See you in a week."

He laughs. "Yes, Marcus, in a week."

One-Eyed Jack backs *Iguana* out and with a toot of her horn, an increase in PPMs (putts per minute), and a puff of smoke, she is gone.

I am alone in the jungle with Katia.

This is awesome.

The early morning sun rises over the island. My immediate concern with my female friend is shelter. The red horizon of the morning sunrise during our drop-off was the suitable warning of a building storm.

Katia is moving about on the sandy beach and building a cooking area. She has the cooking pot suspended over a pile of dry branches and leaves that is cupped by a deep bowl that she dug out of the sand.

The cooking pot is held up by a tripod of sturdy branches. The fire is not yet lit; we will wait for nightfall. The fire is important, not only for food, but a helpful way of warding off our most dangerous enemy in the jungle—the jaguar.

Nothing brings fear into the heart of any human *"en la selva"* than the low-pitched growl of a cat in the dead of night. I am indeed part of that human tribe currently existing under the Amazonian canopy.

Near a tall kapok tree on the island I spot a large, flat area between the crook of its two largest roots. I move over to the beach camp and motion to Katia that I am considering building a tree-house for us. I start to speak in English and pick up the frustrated look on her face and realize she does not understand a word I am saying.

"Marcos, *onde dormimos hoje à noite?*" she asks.

I do not speak Portuguese, but I have learned enough Spanish to get by in Brazil. I know enough to understand her question and answer in broken Portuguese.

"*Nos encampamento na arbole, Katia.*" It is bad grammar but effective.

It helps when I point to the tree with my hammock in hand.

Katia nods in approval and reaches down to her hammock and hands it to me. It is an incredibly soft woven mesh device and it smells like coconut.

She has no rain tarp or mosquito net so I take my shelter equipment and get to work.

I climb the ancient tree easily. Its giant snakelike roots offer wonderful handholds and footholds to get me to a height of approximately twelve feet above the sandy beach. The tree is right on the edge of the forest but far enough on the outside edge to offer protection from the rain yet still get the illumination from the moon and stars.

Deep in the canopy, things become dark and spooky after sunset. This offers us an excellent vantage to observe the comings and goings along the river. This beach is the only suitable landing spot on the 14-acre island.

The giant kapok is by far the most majestic tree in the Amazon rainforest. It grows to heights over 200 feet tall and has a trunk diameter measured in yards, not inches or feet.

This tree looks as if it serves as a marker to the center of the planet. From the waterline, it is obscured by the other trees in the forest, And the top of the tree towers over the surrounding jungle.

I now know why Miguel has left me here. It is a perfect way-point to locate our rendezvous position in case I am lost in the jungle.

The large roots of the tree form a series of blades, similar in shape to a dragon's tail. Each root courses, twists, and turns its way into the earth. I can only imagine how deep they run under the surface.

I find a smooth saddle between two blades that have captured and cradles two fallen palm trees. The lattice forms a perfect frame to tie up our hammocks, suspend a mosi-net over the two beds, and then suspend a rain tarp over the entirety of the camp.

It is perfect.

Once I complete the task I return to the beach and find Katia cleaning and sorting the vegetables for the evening meal.

Later that evening Katia kills the chicken, stuffs it with vegetables, and cooks it over the campfire. She does it with a purpose so we do not lure a jaguar into camp.

Tomorrow I will fish for our protein.

Following our meal, we settle into our hammocks, leaving the fire below burning.

I sling myself in the soft fabric of my bed, suspended between the roots of the large Kapok tree, and watch the moonlight illuminate the flowing water of the river below.

Katia sticks out her leg from her hammock and kicks my hammock, rocking me from side to side in a friendly gesture. We drift off to sleep.

CAMP

DOLPHIN ISLAND

PIRATES

Dolphin Island—Amazon Basin
SPRING 2001
AUTHOR AGE: 34

I awaken in the Amazon, the hazy sun rising above th
palm trees to the east. I climb out of my hammock a
machete. The terrain on that side of the river is low an
sun easily expands over the horizon and rouses me fro
mock at an early hour.

At this particular time, I am wearing nothing
surf shorts, and a fancy watch on my left wrist. It i
Seamaster watch that our sponsor gave each mer
Blakexpeditions crew.

It is 5:14 am.

My wrist is irritated by a persistent rash developi
large titanium body of the timepiece. My skin is raise
circle under the round body of the watch face and is
an eighth of an inch from its surrounding surface. I
watch and let my skin breathe for a little, forcing r
scratch it with the sharp blade of my knife. The last
out here is an open wound and an infection. But it it

I have been trying to treat it with a topical antibi
med kit, but it is obviously a fungus. Katia is still a
climb down the large dragon tail of a root from the g

I find the medical pouch Doc Fullerton built for me years
 and unzip the bag. In the bottom, I have sterilized and pack-
ed waterproof gauze bandages to soak up big bleeds and cover
ge areas, like abdomen or head wounds, medium gauze, and
ious packing gauze to fill wounds, including several tampons,
ich are excellent for puncture wounds or gunshots, or a female
veling companion.

Also in the bottom are wrapping bandages, a cotton sling, and
ious types of tape, including a self-sticking wrapping tape often
d for horses, which is the same flexible waterproof tape I taught
ers to use in SEAL training.

Under the soft patching equipment and the tape is a series of
ckets for hard items such as sterilized scalpels, tweezers, an arte-
 clamp, scissors, a flashlight, and a military grade tourniquet.

On the top flap of my med kit is a set IV bag with a line and
gauge IV needle set wrapped up and taped for easy deployment.
der the IV bag are all my liquids, pills, and pastes.

I move the clear plastic bag of saline solution to the side and
l out my liquid bottles. My four-inch by one-inch vials are
rked appropriately: Alcohol. Peroxide. Iodine. Bleach.

Bingo.

Today I am not messing around with this bloody rash, I am
ng in for the Doc Fullerton fungus kill.

Years ago, Doc taught me to deal with these fungal infections
my feet by soaking them in bleach.

Doc used to tell me, "When in doubt, overload," then dousing
with bleach.

I do the same this morning.

Pain.

It feels delicious, the searing pain of something that had to be
rking because it hurts sooo bad.

Unfortunately, in my agony I wake Katia up and she giggles
my dilemma. There is not a scratch on her body, she just floats
ss this terrain.

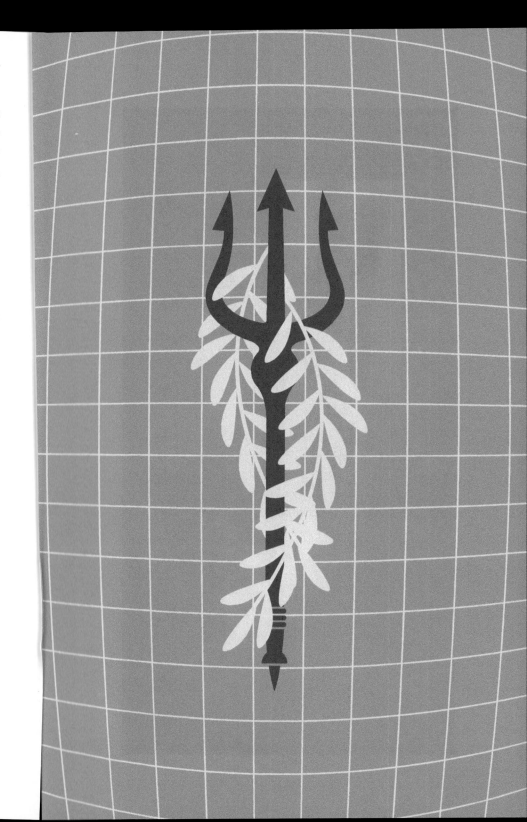

I try to do the same, but there is always something down here reminding me that I am very much human.

When I finish wrapping my wound with a piece of gauze, I look down to the river below the old Kapok and beyond the white sand of our little beach.

The air is clear and crisp in the mornings here. It's refreshing. Often it is excessively muggy in the night and uncomfortable to sleep. I usually dust myself with baby powder from my rucksack each night before I sleep. It keeps my body dry and my hammock clean from sweat. It is also very much a treat…simple pleasures.

If you have the luxury, mornings are the best time to sleep, when the air is cooler. Today the air is unusually cool and it has created a mist over the brownish surface of the Roosevelt. Through the mist I spot a boat approaching our island. It is floating downstream from the south, one figure on the bow of an eighteen-foot dugout canoe.

The figure is a large male and he has a long pole in his hands, pushing the boat into the shallows of our beach. I can make out two more figures in the boat behind him, both males. They appear younger than the man up front.

The boat is full of bags, or packages, on top of which are several nets and freshly caught fish.

I see all three men clearly as the bow plows up on the white sand some fifty yards away from my position up in the tree. The men do not see me.

They are wearing long pants and tall lace-up boots…snake boots. This is interesting to me, since fishermen are traditionally dressed in nothing but shorts and a pair of plastic flip-flops. As a matter of fact, the slang word for these fishermen in the Amazon is "flip flops."

The fact that these men are plying the river in boots implies they are spending more time in the jungle than on the river. These are not your typical fishermen.

Cautiously, I put my $4,000 watch into the med kit and zip it closed. I will end up keeping it there for the rest of my time in the Amazon.

I turn up to our tree camp and see Katia settling into her hammock, she pops her head out and gives me a knowing look. She whispers one word to me, and the way she says it gives me chills.

"Cabocles."

Cabocles is slang for a certain type of river people in the Amazon. They are a mixed breed of the inhabitants to the basin that comes from the original Portuguese explorers and settlers mixing with the local Indios to produce a biracial society. Indios down here are known to keep immaculate settlements and respect the jungle biosphere. Portuguese are known to be focused on trade along the waterways.

Cabocles are known to be neither.

Cabocles are the multitude that live on the river and throw their trash and pollute with a complete disregard to nature. They kill what they want for sport or trifle. As an example, they enjoy capturing the endangered sea turtles of the region and cooking them alive in their shells, just because it makes a nice stew.

Cabocles are the ones burning down hundreds of acres of forest so that they may raise a few heads of cattle in the wasteland.

I know well what Katia means when she dips back under her covers. I slide over to the backside of the tree so the men do not see me climb from our tree house. I make a large semi-circle in the forest and emerge from the eastern side of the island, walking along the beach where I had encountered the Pesci boas.

The men see me and do not even register me with a greeting. They make their way to our cooking camp.

All of the men are shirtless, and each of them has a shotgun slung upside down over their right shoulders. All three are covered in dark tattoos that are indecipherable against the contrast of their dark, weathered skin.

The two younger men are in their early twenties, the older in his thirties. The older man leads the way and finds a seat at the cooking camp.

The two others sit behind him in the sand, lay their shotguns in their laps to keep them out of the sand, lean back on their elbows, and cross their feet.

The older man pokes his fingers into my cooking pot and scoops out a bit of vegetable and chicken from the night before. I approach the men and adjust myself to their brazen approach to camp.

I am obviously on their turf. I adapt myself to their energy and make my actions clear with body language. I square my shoulders and approach them as if I have expected them to do exactly what they have done. I sit down on a log in the sand across from the leader and plant my machete between my legs in the sand, not threateningly. I hold it as if I just finished hacking through ten miles of jungle, the sharp edge out toward the leader.

The edge is clean and sharp; I know he will notice. I am not a simple tourist.

The morning breeze flows off the river and it carries the smell of sweat, alcohol, and tobacco to my nose. These are dirty men.

The leader's hair is dark, a thick mat that obscures his eyes until they peer out at me. They are lifeless eyes, dull, the brown irises seeming to hover in the upper crest of his eyeball. He reminds me of a shark.

He reminds me of a pirate.

I can cut the leader's throat with my large blade and use his shotgun on the other two before they get off of their elbows.

The leader has an Ithaca 37 pump-action 12 gauge with a single barrel. It is a dangerous weapon. It fires as quick as he can pump the action. This was a weapon of choice for SEALs in Vietnam for its durability in the jungle.

Violence of action.

I think of the approach to battle with my mentor, Doc Fullerton, when he led us into Close Quarters Battle. Violence of Action is simply attacking with a direct and focused assault, and never giving up.

Doc famously told Charlie Platoon, "When in doubt, overload."

If I make a move this morning to defend Katia and myself, it will be swift, decisive, and unrelenting. It will be focused on getting control of that Ithaca.

The man pokes his finger in my cooking pot and licks it. He moves like a serpent, and he talks like one too. I do not like this man.

"Você cozinhou isso?" He asks me if this is my cooking in Portuguese. I understand because of the similarity to Spanish words.

"Eu cozinhou esso." I confirm that it is my cooking, not a female's, then interject, *"No Portuguesa, habla Español."*

A young man behind the leader speaks up in English. "Not necessary. You American?"

"Yeah, I'm from California."

"Boss wants to know if you are alone."

"Just me," I answer.

"You surf?"

"Yeah, in southern California mostly."

"Cool, I surf too. I'm from Recife."

"Dude, I surfed Recife. Good waves down there. I surfed Pyramid Rock. I love the lefts off the point."

"Yeah, we call that the wedge, like you have up in Newport Beach. What were you doing in Recife?"

"I was in the military. I was training the Brazilian Navy SEALs there."

"I surfed in my off-time up at Recife."

I am careful with saying I was in the military, or in Special Forces. In Colombia, you would be prime kidnapping material with the FARC rebels, so you never admit such things. Down here, it is more about letting them know I will put up a good fight if they want to mess with me.

The young man speaks in Portuguese to this crew, telling them I am *"militar."*

"Boss wants to know why you are back here," he asks me.

The older man saddles his shotgun in his lap as if it is a pet.

"I am scouting for a TV show for National Geographic."

"No shit?" says the boy.

The older man gets the vibe and picks up on it. "Nat Geo!" he exclaims.

"Cool, what are you scouting here?"

"Right now, just good places to spot Cayman and film the piranha. I'm hoping you guys might direct me to some tributaries that are worth exploring. Tell me where I do not want to go."

After conferring among the three men, the leader gave directions to the English speaker.

"Boss says to stay away from the eastern shore of Arapui. There is a highway to the east that runs along the river. You don't want anything to do with the tributaries over there, *comprende, militar?*"

"Great info."

"Boss says good fishing in the quiet lagoons on the west bank here. You're in a good spot. He wants to know if you are alone."

"I have a scouting vessel ahead getting supplies and a seaplane overhead if I need it. I'm working with the governor's office out of Manaus so I get all I need."

I am totally bullshitting, in a calculating way.

"I don't have much out here," I say jumping the conversation ahead. "I can use fresh fish for the next few days if you guys want to trade."

"You have money?" the young man asks.

"No money." I go to my beach cache Katia and I buried last night.

Safe in a woven basket I have our vegetables and fruit, the remainder of the chicken Katia jerked, and the cooked gut pieces I will use for piranha bait later.

I pull out the bottle of whiskey. "How about I trade you this bottle for some of your fish? In the meantime, I will make sure to scout to the west and not bother with the eastern side of the river."

The leader nods in approval and signals the boys to get in the boat. I follow the two young men as the leader has one more look around and then thankfully follows us back to the dugout.

"What are you doing up here away from the surf, brother?" I ask the young man.

"I used to be a police officer down there. Better money up here in the rivers right now. Just watch your back around here. It gets more dangerous as you travel south."

"I was thinking about running to the Pareces and the diamond mines down there with the Cinta Larga."

"No, you don't want to go down there. It's all blown out, it's ugly."

"My other choice is up north to the Rio Negro."

"Go north, be careful in Manuas." he says.

"Thanks."

I make my decision on the spot, but plan to speak with Miguel when he returns. I have a good feeling I will know his answer as well. Until then, I will be careful to keep Katia safe and move our camp back into the forest so as not to invite other such inquiries.

After they leave, I return to the safety of the large Kapok tree and find Katia.

"Marco, *piratas*."

"Huh?"

"*Drogas, assassinos, ladrões*...Marco."

"Let's set a camp in the forest until Miguel arrives, it's a bit dangerous down here."

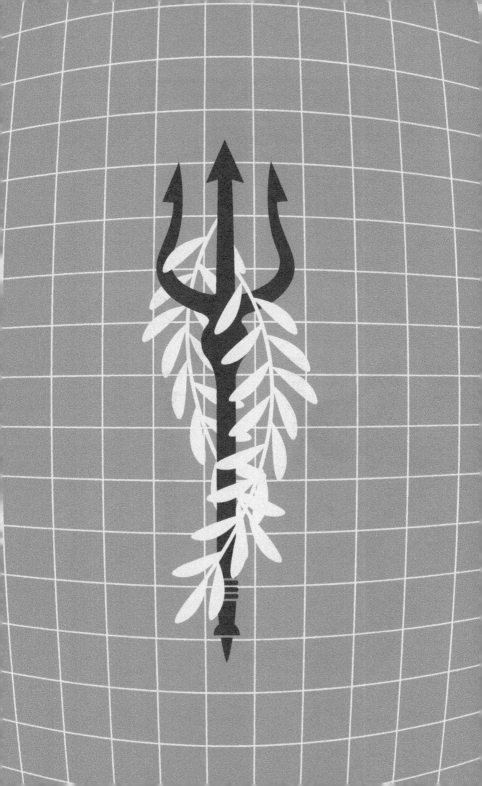

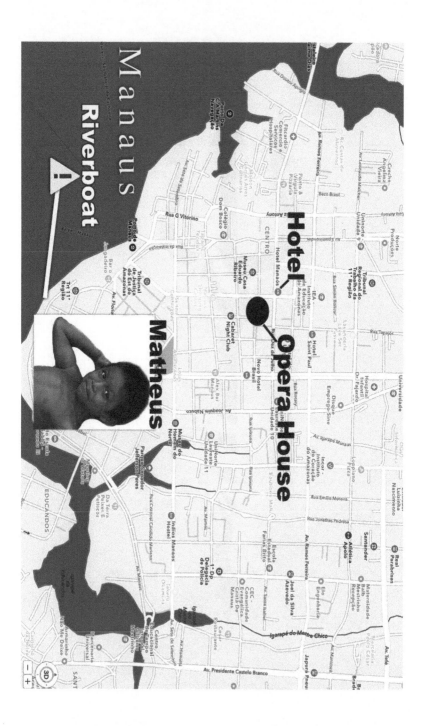

THE ORPHANS OF MANAUS

The Rio Negro, Brazil
SPRING 2001
AUTHOR AGE: 34

Miguel's return from Via do Campo is on time and his response to my concerns is predictable.

We decide that we will explore the River of Tea and instead follow Jacques-Yves Cousteau's route to the Casiquiare River of Venezuela, by way of the Rio Negro.

When we first arrive in the jungle metropolis of Manaus, I insist I stay at a hotel in the center of the city near the old Opera House.

It is a fascinating structure. It was built in the days of Teddy Roosevelt's adventures in the region, originally designed to entertain the rubber barons and elite that were the early exploiters of the Amazon Basin in the early nineteen hundreds. The building still stands in all its glory.

My time with Miguel down south on the Roosevelt taught me a lot about his efforts as a charitable person.

Miguel was extremely aware of two key factors of utmost importance to him.

He makes a point of helping impoverished indigenous communities, and he also sets up protective shelters for the ever present flow of young indigenous children from the surrounding jungle.

Whether they were orphaned or running from abuse by the onslaught of the Cabocles invading more and more of the jungle, these kids would end up on the streets of this sprawling city in the heart of the Amazon itself.

Miguel is concerned about these kids and it is obvious.

He confides to me that he has built a community up the Rio Negro to keep them out of the city and closer to the forest and their culture. The town is called Novo Airão. Miguel made me aware of these lost children of the forest scattered throughout the city. They were everywhere.

During a time Miguel had to travel upriver, I would explore Manaus and see them gathering in parks and old buildings, hiding in trees along the busy streets, and, sadly, watching the uniformed school kids of the city play in their protected playgrounds.

I thought a lot about the movie *Oliver Twist* and can see many similarities. It is as if they have set up their own counterculture behind the scenes of the busy city.

Miguel also made me aware of the Cabocles exploiting them as well.

As I was seeing in the Roosevelt River to the south, the drug trade is at an insidious beginning in this once virgin region of the rainforest.

What is starting in the streets of cities much farther south and on the beautiful coastal beaches of Rio and Recife is spreading to this region with a speed that I, unfortunately, do not recognize in this scouting mission for Sir Peter.

Had I been more informed of the evil overtaking this region I may have saved a precious life.

Driving the streets of Manaus, I do not see the evil sweeping in like a dark tide.

It is similar to the depiction in the JRR Tolkien tale of *The Hobbit* and *The Fellowship of the Ring*. The surrounding forest is slowly dying. Dark clouds are on the horizon, and unlike the wizard Gandalf, I am not able to see these early signs.

On this night I am about to learn a valuable lesson.

While I am out exploring, I end up getting pulled over and shaken down with a gun to my head by some local police.

The affair is intimidating. I end up losing the cash in my pockets, but I break the ice by conversing in Spanish when they ask me what I am doing in the city.

"Nat Geo!" is the key response from them after I answer their question. I walk them to my trunk and show them my helmet camera after I feel we connected a little bit and we talk about the adventure. I tell them I am looking for a good story to tell on film. The strategy works, and one of the cops insists I meet his cousin that runs a local hotel. He makes it very clear when he drops me off in the cop car.

"Tonight, you stay here."

I do as I am told.

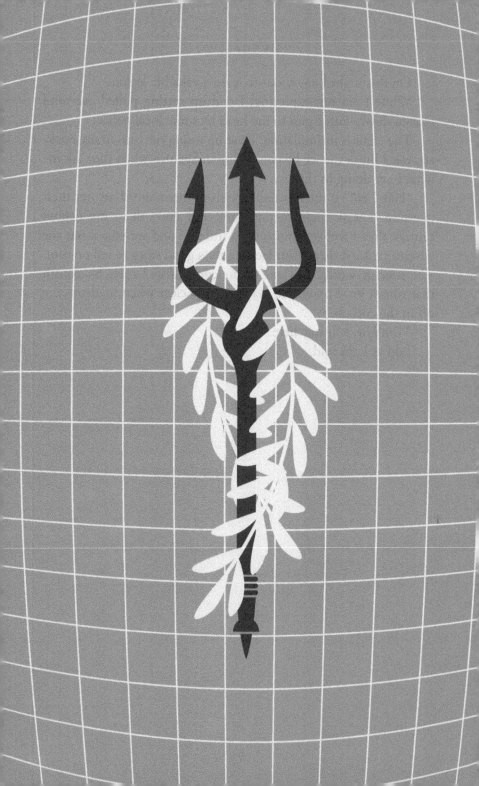

KNOCK ON THE DOOR

Manaus, Brazil
SPRING 2001
AUTHOR AGE: 34

At some point in the night, there is a knock on the door.

I am confident it is a prostitute with a scalpel in her hand to retrieve my liver.

I do not answer the door.

The knocks continue on the metal barrier that protects me from the dirty hallway.

A voice on the other side, the soft voice of a woman speaks in English, "Open the door, adventure man."

Not by the hair on my chinny-chin-chin.

Then curiosity gets the better of me. I reluctantly crack the door open, only slightly. There is no security chain so I wedge the soft rubber of my boot in the tiny gap between it and the smooth tiles of the floor for extra security.

"Are you alone?" I ask with great trepidation, taking in the dark figure in hallway.

She has a large set of beautiful brown eyes and long flowing hair as black as a raven.

She has the eyes of a wolf. "I am," she answers.

I open the gap from one inch to three.

My gaze drifts from her eyes to her ruby-colored lips, then her neck and throat. I am seeing the beauty of a woman, but feel a tinge of reluctance with my hormones.

Something is not quite feminine about her. She looks to be in her mid-thirties, about my age. It is not her age that throws me off a bit, but her neck…it's strong.

Too strong.

I trace lower to a strong set of shoulders, then arms, and a hard, flat belly under a dark-colored tank top. The inverted triangle frames a set of small breasts, so that part checks out.

Keep your cool, Marco.

Lower, my gaze reveals a pair of cut-off Daisy Duke jean shorts, dark, smooth legs, and a pair of blue flip-flops padding her ruby-colored toenails.

"You like?" she asks me, staring into my eyes from the dark and dirty hallway.

"I'm not here to like, I'm here to survive the night."

"I know, adventurer, my cousin dropped you off with me."

"This is your place?"

"Yes, welcome to the Hotel California."

"You let me in."

I groan.

"You don't like?"

"Nonononono, I just mean the situation sucks. I don't want trouble, and I know that freaking song by the Eagles."

The woman pushes herself into my room. I think back to harmonizing the song many times with Doc Fullerton and the entire Charlie platoon in our trips to South America. We played it at many a campfire training Special Forces soldiers across the continent.

When the woman brushes past my position in the door I smell coconut and tanning oil. She definitely takes care of herself and is well preened. Her skin is perfect and her hair looks like something from a shampoo commercial.

Somehow she seems taller now that she is in my room. We stare at each other at eye level. It is more of a face-off than the gaze of potential lovers, not that that would happen. Even so, this is different. I am sizing her up more for a fight than a love session.

I puff up my chest and project a bit and she responds the same.

She's a man.

I knew it.

"My name is Roxana, and you are safe here."

"You landed yourself in the middle of something here in Manaus, Mr. Marcos."

"You speak great English, Roxana. I appreciate that. I had a tough time with your cousin."

"You are an explorer, yes?" she asks.

"Yeah. We're going to be filming an expedition for Nat Geo Channel up here, if I survive this scouting mission."

I sit across from my newfound friend and notice a cross on her necklace.

"You're Catholic?" I ask.

"Not in the traditional sense, but I grew up that way, and I consider myself a Catholic, even though I am shunned by others in the faith."

"I get it, Roxy. You know, when my little brother, Luke, died, the priest wouldn't let me bring his ashes in the church for his own service, so I snuck him in."

"There is a lot of selective judgement going on in the church, but I keep God here in my heart."

"How long are you here in Manaus?"

"I have a couple weeks here. My guide is taking another group upriver, so I am researching filming subjects here in the city."

"We have a story for you."

She shakes her head. "Our story must be told on TV, Marcos. It's too ugly for the world not to know."

"Who exactly are you referring to?" I ask, curious about her meaning of the word "our" in this context.

"We are. *Os Indesejáveis.*"

The word is new to me. "In-de-shahvez?"

"The Undesirables, Marcos. We are the unwanted of society, children of the streets, the lost children of the forest. We are alone here and we are dying. Many children, the old and the sick, and many like myself." Roxy motions her hands over her body. Her posture is perfect until her final words, when she slumps, as if a burden is released from her shoulders.

Roxy looks up at me. The features of her face are both male and female. There is a deep compassion in her eyes, no matter the gender identification.

"We hear you are filming Nat Geo here. We need your help."

"Me? Oh no, *chica*, I don't need any trouble here in Manaus. That's the only instructions I got from my guide, Miguel, and my girlfriend, Katia." I threw the last bit in for extra measure. "Is it money?" I ask.

"No, Marcos it is safety. There are many against us."

"Gangs? *Los maras?*" I ask.

"Worse than the gangs. These are vigilantes."

Roxy opens a tattered envelope and shows me black and white photos of children and transgender prostitutes slaughtered in the streets of the city, they are chopped into pieces. Some have messages carved into their skin. This is extremely disturbing to me. She slides the photos back in the envelope. "I am sorry to be so blunt, but our time is limited to persuade you to make this your story."

"Why show me those pictures?"

"Because that is what they are doing to the children, the old, and the gays on the streets."

"Who are 'they?'"

"They are called *Os Martires*, The Martyrs. Someone is paying them to clean the streets of what they call *Os Indesejáveis*." She moves to open the envelope again and I sit upright on my stool.

"No, please, I understand." I put my hands over hers to stop her.

"If you film this story it will force awareness. I hear they are using gang members from *Familia do Norte* as scouts. Those are the ones with the face tattoos." Roxy makes a motion across her face and neck, then pulls out a few pictures of the gang members bearing the familiar markings. The crew I met on the River of Doubt back at Dolphin Island had the same markings. "These are the most dangerous in the city, Marcos."

I push the photos back to her. Something in the back of my head does not feel right about this endeavor. But I am about to involve myself in a very dangerous battle.

"I want to take you to a secret hiding place tomorrow night. We will travel with my friend, Zella."

"Where is it?" I ask.

"The old docks, it is where we hide the street children, you can film this, it is a very powerful story."

"You're on."

Later in the day, I had a phone conversation with Sir Peter, who was now in Buenos Aires, Argentina, and beginning to refit the *Seamaster* for the jungle.

He told me that they are designing a canvas canopy to cover the entire deck to give us shade and protection from the rain as the vessel makes her way up the Amazon.

Sir Peter was curious about the Amazon journey and what I felt we had to share about our current location.

I gave him some contact information in case I had an emergency while Miguel is out and away, as is the case at the moment.

I also told him I would check in with Doc Fullerton.

I informed my captain that I am doing some research on Manaus for our storyline. I left out the part about transgender prostitutes and vigilante gangs for the moment.

I did however tell Doc Fullerton when I got him on the phone. I believe it took Doc at least twenty minutes to stop laughing. Being the platoon chief that he is, he already has contact information for when he has to bail me out of jail.

"That's the classic Breeze right there," he laughs. "You are knee deep in hand grenade pins and transgender prostitutes, fighting the world's battles and making a difference out there, one life at a time. I got your back, Breeze."

"Thanks, Doc."

"Yeah, well, don't thank me so quick. I am tellin' your mom what you're up to out there. You just remember to always make her proud, you copy?"

"Yes, Doc."

"Be safe, Marco. I'm proud of you, don't forget it."

"Aye, Senior Chief."

11pm
Manaus, Brazil

When my Seamaster watch strikes the hour, Roxy and her tall friend appear on the horizon of our meeting spot near the opera house. They are surrounded by a group of street children. The two men look like a mystical band of forest elves who appear and disappear at will. The two wait in the shadows as Roxy signals me in.

I gather my belongings and make my goodbyes to an old woman I was sharing time with. She gives me a blessing of sorts even though we never share a word. The old woman gives me a powerful embrace, reinforcing that the Indios do, indeed, have a lack of personal space. I love it. During the night she was picking through my hair, perhaps looking for a snack. I was glad to disappoint.

The children circle me while Roxy introduces me to her friend.

Inside the circle, I am hit with the striking features of Zella.

Zella has similar features to Roxy, and even Katia. Roxy confirms they are all from the same region of the River of Doubt that Teddy Roosevelt had explored, where many of the Indio women are trained to be Carnival dancers. Not surprisingly, these men in front of me obviously take it to the extremes and emulate the beautiful women of their region, actually quite well.

Both of them in their high heels are taller than me, so it is really freaky.

Zella is extremely stoic and quiet, like a silent forest sentinel. Both look potentially lethal, if crossed. I treat each of them with respect, but focus on Roxy as the leader, and stay out of their wolf pack.

"Where do we go, Roxy?"

"The children have gathering areas for each of us. Zella will bring in her pack while we move to the docks."

"The docks?"

"Yes, we walk from here to the Rio Negro and the old riverboats. We all live on a floating city. It is the safest place in Manaus for us after midnight."

"What happens after midnight?"

"The gangs come out. And so do the vigilantes."

Zella splits off and walks down a separate path as I follow Roxy.

She walks quickly, like a cat through a putrid alley. There is trash scattered in the street behind several restaurants and a homeless person rummages through bottles and cans behind a nightclub. There is a homeless man heating up some type of drug in a soda can and inhaling its fumes to get high. We cross his path without any indication he even notices our presence.

Dogs scurry under foot and disappear, and long-tailed rats scamper in dark corners.

I have seen worse in the back alleys of Olongapo, in the Philippines, but that is another story entirely, from my Marine Corps days, before I became a SEAL.

"How far to the river, Roxy?"

"One mile. We each take separate roads to the south... Sarmiento, Ribiero, and Barroso. These all lead to the river road Manaus Moderna."

"How many do you have?" I ask.

"Eight of us total. I still have to pick up mine."

"Why don't you stay at Hotel California?"

"Too dangerous, Marcos. If the business owners saw the children in and out we would all be killed within days. I have my three waiting ahead."

As we round a corner Roxy matches up with her children who were hiding behind an old dumpster. "When we split up it is harder to follow us home," Roxy explains, giving the two girls and the boy a big hug.

"Are you being watched?"

"We believe so."

The two girls stay by Roxy. The boy moves to my side and offers me his hand. The pipsqueak is no bigger than a mouse, probably six years old.

"*Explorador*," he says.

"*Passarinho*," I say and he smiles. I take his tiny hand into mine.

"His name is Matheus," Roxy tells me.

The gesture and the feeling remind me of my time as an EMT when I had to pick up a fetus a young woman aborted in a hospital emergency room. She dropped her underwear on the floor after we brought her in on a 911 call and there it was. The nurses handled the woman, and I bent down to pick up the baby, no bigger than the palm of my hand. I felt its tiny ribs in my hand, and then touching the tiny bones in his or her hand. I almost passed out at the sensation.

I take the boy's hand and he guides me through the streets of Manaus. He squeezes my right hand tight and tears well up in my eyes.

I am now traveling the secret path of the undesirables with a little friend.

We make our way across four blocks to the south of the opera house, on Barosso Street. Roxy crosses us at 7 September Street and we connect to Deodoro Street, now moving southwest for several blocks. We cross the highway BR 174 and meet the other pack members in a large dirt parking lot on the river's edge.

Roxy does a head count and we all move across the riverfront street called Moderna and onto a large rundown dock structure.

There are abandoned boats *everywhere*. It is like a graveyard of Amazonian riverboats, I have never seen anything like it.

Somehow we skirted past all of this with Miguel's boat *Iguana*, and I did not notice, but I do now because I am about to sleep in one of these tonight.

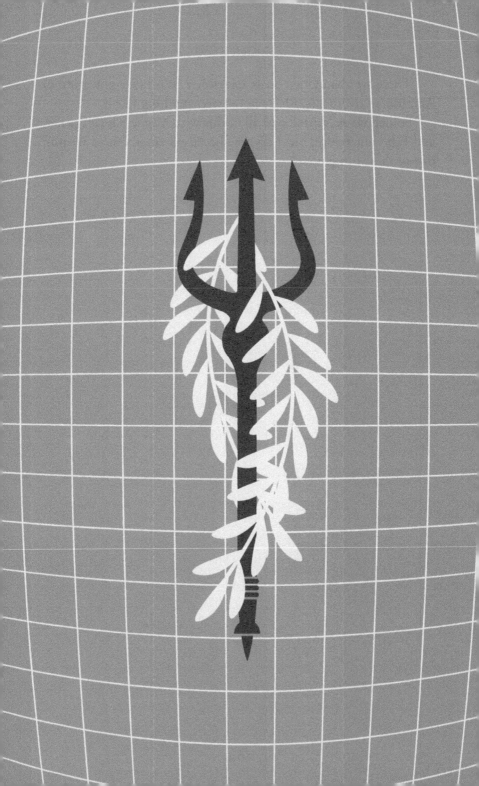

ENCANTADO

Amazon River Boat, Rio Negro
Manaus, Brazil
SPRING 2001
AUTHOR AGE: 34

Roxy guides me, along with the rest of the gang, to the large dou-ble-decker riverboat that they call home.

The procession to the boat is quite festive down at the river's edge, and the waterfront puts everyone at ease in comparison to the hustle of the city.

Zella and her children end up down at the water where they jump in the water and bathe while others move up the beach and go to the bathroom.

There are many boats with overhanging decks and simple holes in the floor that drop down into the water for the boat people to do their business. I avoid the water.

I follow Roxy with her two girls up a wooden plank and into the belly of the beached whale. The two girls, each about eight to ten years old, never leave Roxy's sight.

I hold on to Matheus. I like his name because he reminds me of my own little brother, Matthew.

It's funny, because I see each of my little brothers in other members in this gang of orphans.

Roxy unlocks a wooden double door and opens up a large cav-ernous room on the top enclosed deck of the vessel. The riverboat is at least two hundred feet long. It is huge! At one time it must have been a river ferry to the cities that I hear about upriver.

There is no electricity or water on the craft, but it provides a comfortable living space with open wooden slat windows allowing a fresh breeze off the river to lift away the dense humidity of the city.

As my eyes adjust to the ambient light of the moon that penetrates the open windows, I see hammocks everywhere.

Zella brings in a flickering kerosene lamp and illuminates the room. I shudder at the thought of a gas lamp in a wooden boat full of children. The boat smells like an ancient ship, and the river breeze keeps it cool.

Roxy and Zella gather together and obviously talk about me, pointing as they make comments, but it all seems casual.

Zella goes to a galley and brings out a bag of fruit for the collective and forms them in a circle, sitting around the gas lamp.

Matheus brings me into the circle and I sit cross-legged near the children. There is a little girl I call Quiet Bird. She is staring into the flame of the burning lamp right now as if she is on a different planet.

Zella starts talking to the group during what she calls story time, while Roxy sits by my side, helping me translate.

Zella points to me and says, "*Encantado.*"

The room gasps in a collective shriek. Three of the little girls get up and run around the room, some pointing at me.

"What did I do?" I ask Roxy.

The two Roxy girls laugh, latching on to Roxy. All of the boys laugh hysterically, clearly at me.

Zella collects Quiet Bird back to the makeshift campfire and Roxy translates her story to the calmed group.

Apparently, I am an *Encantado*, a shapeshifter. By day I am a pink river dolphin; at night, the legend of the pink dolphin turns into a man and walks ashore to seduce the women of the village.

Zella describes the river dolphin sometimes kidnapping the women of the village and dragging them into the river and back to the magical place called Encante.

"*Encantado* is the enchanted one. He comes from an underwater realm called the Encante. In human form he is pale-skinned and graceful, usually dressed in earth-colored clothes in an old-fashioned style."

All the children scream.

Roxy explains that many villages actually have a logbook where mother and father are entered for each child, and if they want to hide the true father, they simply say Boto, for dolphin.

Some of these children in the room actually grew up thinking their father was a dolphin!

Just to rub it in, Roxy says, "Encantados are said to be fond of music and abducting humans and taking them back to the land of Encante."

And here I am, the pink dolphin.

The whole story makes for a crazy event aboard the once abandoned ship.

I am glad I have become such a great stage prop for the prostitutes and the children, at least for one night.

Roxy invites me to tell a story to the group while she translates. I keep the theme going, and I tell them about the place where I grew up, Dolphin Island. I tell them how I would swim off the shore, turn into a human, and come up on the beach to my friend who lives in the solitary tree of the island.

When I finish my story, I have the attention of everyone in the room.

The group moves towards their hammocks and turns in for the night. There are many giggles throughout the process of deciding where I am going to sleep.

"How do you keep this place for yourselves?" I ask Roxy. "It seems like the other homeless would be swarming this place."

"No one messes with us, Marcos. They know who we are and what we do to the ones who cross us."

I do not reply, but I am concerned. If they know who you are, they know where you are. This is not a secure location.

I end up finding a hammock surrounded by the Forest Elves, which makes all the children feel more comfortable about the stranger in their midst. I was a bit mad at Zella for calling me the Encantado and scaring the children, but I roll with it.

I end up sleeping well for most of the night, but I wake up around 3 am to Roxy's hand on my shoulder. She is still in her hammock and she wakes me up to patrol the vessel.

We take a walk outside the main room and make our way up a stairwell to the roof and sit for about an hour under the moon, talking.

Before we head back, Zella comes up and joins us. I sit in a semi-circle with them while Roxy interprets a conversation between all of us.

I find the transgender men interesting; it is as if there is a child trapped in each of them that screams to find the age of innocence again. There are the male instincts to hunt and kill, yet the feminine instincts to nurture and protect.

I put it all into the context of storyboarding our Nat Geo Amazon adventure. This is fascinating to witness, a subculture I call The Children of the Forest, being forced from the natural world to survive in the concrete jungle built in the center of the last remaining rainforests of South America. The story highlights the beauty of nature and the impact of man.

My thoughts are interrupted by a large rat running a few inches from my arm. *Ewww.*

Zella quietly walks to the edge of the boat on the port side. We are up near the stern of the vessel and she signals for us to come to her.

We hear the sound of men moving below.

I stalk to the edge of the roof and observe three men loitering on the open deck of the stern below us. They are covered in tattoos, and they appear to be attempting stealth.

Roxy grips my shoulder and whispers in my ear, *"Piratas."*

That is the last word I thought I would hear in the Amazon jungle, let alone this particular century, but this is now my reality. My heart moves up into my throat, and for a moment I can only hear the thump of my increasing heartbeat in the back of my ear canal.

This is real.

I shift out of Nat Geo storyline mode and into fear mode. I feel incredibly vulnerable in this situation. There are no rules out here; I am alone, away from my fellow warriors and teammates, there is no backup, and I am unarmed.

The transgender men are barefoot, and they maneuver quietly down the access stairs and back into the sleeping quarters. I follow their lead.

I know they have street skills, but I do not put my life in depending on that. I begin actively planning on a defense strategy that includes me and the children if need be.

Roxy pushes our team into the berthing area of hammocks and children, then barricades the double door shut from inside with a mahogany plank.

Zella moves to the galley area and opens a compartment under the deck planks near the cabinets of the cooking area. She pulls out two pistols.

Roxy's friend hands me a rusty Colt 1911 .45 pistol. I aim it in a safe direction and inspect it. The gun has one rusty metal magazine in the handle. I cock the slide back with a pull resisted by grinding corrosion. *Not good.*

I catch a brass .45 round as it pops out of the chamber and into my palm. I pop the magazine release on the pistol grip with my right thumb and tap the side of the weapon to ease it out. It is stuck in the pistol grip well.

I move to my knees, pull the weapon into my sternum, and keep it directed at a safe area in the back of the room.

Roxy and Zella corral the children up near the bow area of the berthing room we are in, then move to the door.

Roxy moves to me. "You stay here and protect the children."

Initially, I am ass-burnt because I like to be out on point in a threatening situation, and I don't like the idea of huddling behind the women. But then again, these are not actually—

"Marcos!" Roxy snaps me back to the moment. "Guard the children."

"I got it, Roxy. Are you sure?"

"Yes. This is for me to handle. This is trouble. They are river pirates."

"Got it, Roxy. Be safe."

I want my SEAL Team gear on me, I want a primary weapon and a backup weapon, I want a radio and teammates. I want Doc Fullerton and Charlie Platoon by my side.

All I have is a rusty weapon and a jammed magazine.

Mentally, I go back to BUD/S Class 207 and my lesson learned, tying five knots, and talk myself through the evolution.

Don't panic.

You have air, Marco. Breathe.

My class leader, Sam, used to tell me, *one evolution at a time, stay in the moment…not the past. Right here and right now.*

The world is scrambling around me with little kids in one direction, Roxy and Zella moving to the double door, and pirates on the other side.

I go back to the countless tap, rack, bang drills that Doc Fullerton forced all of us in Charlie Platoon to do over and over and over during our close quarters battle training.

I had done it so much that every action was completely automatic, like playing a piano song while there is a bar fight going on around me.

Sitting in the ship's galley, I collect myself and tap the weapon to try to clear the magazine.

The slide of the upper receiver is locked to the rear at the moment, exposing the chamber where the round will slide in and be seated to be fired down the barrel from the magazine below. With the slide to the rear, I tap the side of the gun to drop the magazine.

Nothing happens.

I strike the weapon sharply with the palm of my left hand. This forces the upper receiver forward and it in turn forces a round from the magazine into the chamber in an awkward angle. The round is jammed between the rusty magazine, the upper receiver, and the chamber.

"Marcos, the children!" Roxy whisper-shouts, her eyes wide.

BREATHE!

One evolution at a time.

Clear the weapon, Marco.

I tap the mag from the bottom of the pistol grip and it loosens and pops into place, I slide the receiver back and pop out the jammed round, the next round slides into the chamber perfectly.

It works!

I grab the expended round from the deck, drop the mag and load it and the other while I test the spring and then seat the mag back in the pistol grip. This gives me seven rounds in the weapon.

I know I have one round in the chamber. I put the weapon on safe.

I get up and I move to the children.

Roxy gives me one more glance before she opens the double door.

She leaves the threshold of the open door like a warrior going to battle, and locks us inside the room.

MARCO AND THE PIRATES

Amazon Riverboat, Rio Negro
Manaus, Brazil
SPRING 2001
AUTHOR AGE: 34

Huddling with the group of orphans behind me, I hear Zella clashing with the pirates outside the door. There is a deluge of yelling, which reminds me of hearing the homeless people fight in the back parking lots of the surfing beaches I would visit in San Diego, back in the States. They were often squabbling about whose spot under the bushes is whose, defending turf in crass and vulgar manners. It strikes me that I am comfortable with the way Roxy handles herself, but I never tested Zella. She is an unknown.

I am uncomfortable with the entire affair, and doubt really starts creeping in about being on the wrong side of the door, but I know that a white boy who barely speaks Portuguese will only make things worse out there. I am best suited out of sight unless it is a direct fight, then it is game on.

The thought of exploring the Lost World and indigenous tribes away from this city begins to make a lot more sense to me for a TV show plot. Now it creeps in. What have I gotten myself into?

Outside, the drama unfolds into more shouting from the surrounding boats as more spectators join in and taunt the growing scuffle outside on our decks. Roxy and Zella are taking far too long to conclude the encounter peacefully. I begin to hear sirens in the city nearby. It's turning into a ghetto brawl. Those never end well.

Next to me, the children huddle with each other, and Matheus takes my left hand. I am determined to hold my ground with the kids and give my life if need be in their defense. I will not let anything outside the door come in unless it is our team.

Outside, a scuffle breaks out on the other side of the double doors and I hear the thud of bodies locked in physical combat, punctuated by the scream of a transgender male. The sound is primal and guttural. It sounds like Zella making most of the noise.

I think about putting my rusty gun in the fight, but there are too many variables. I'm locked in this room, I don't have a clear shot, what if the weapon jams? All hell would break loose inside this room full of children. I hold my defensive position. It is not the only choice I have, but I will engage only as a last resort.

POW!

One shot from outside the door. I hear a gasping groan and the gurgling sound of a forced breath, then all is quiet.

I hold my ground and ensure no one breaks through the door.

I hear nothing except the wail of police sirens closing in on the docks. All hell breaks loose.

Oh shit. Dear Lord, what have I gotten myself into?

I am locked inside with the children when the cop cars outside converge. I do not know what kind of raid is coming my way with the children. If these cops are bad we are all in trouble. Even if they are good, I am still in big trouble.

The sirens and thumping boots mean the police or whoever they are will be charging through this boat locked and loaded and potentially ready to kill any undesirable they encounter. Man or woman, boy or girl.

Shifting gears, there is no longer a need to lay low and be quiet. I start hiding the children.

All along the deck is a series of wooden vented cubbyholes that are about eighteen inches tall and three feet wide. I open the double doors by pushing down on a brass latch in the center. One at a time, I stuff children in while the nerve-wracking noise continues outside.

I am simply numb with the idea of going to jail for being associated with what just happened. This is extremely foreign to me, as it is not a direct confrontation with an enemy combatant. This is law enforcement that can take away my freedom, which is worse than death.

The best thing to do is hide.

I start to slide into the last cubbyhole with Matheus. I find an old pair of underwear near my face and tuck the pistol into the dirty cloth, stashing it into a nook, out of his reach. It is a liability now.

The sound of heavy boots and men yelling in Portuguese outside is deafening as I look for a space to fit my body. It is like trying to squeeze into a suitcase.

I am beginning to understand that tonight my mission inside this room is not about me. If I hide, I make the children vulnerable to a search.

"Fuck this," I say out loud to Matheus.

I make the decision not to hide tonight. I crawl out onto the center of the floor where we told our stories earlier. It is best if they find me right away instead of going on a search. I make my move and slide myself to the clear area on the deck after I signal Matheus to sit still and not make a sound. I put my hands on my head with my face to the floor.

GOD'S CHILDREN

Manaus, Brazil
SPRING 2001
AUTHOR AGE: 34

When the police first hit the deck of the riverboat, I know instantly they are not local law enforcement officers.

These are Federal Officers in complete SWAT gear. I have been on the other side of these types of raids. This is a non-permissive environment, meaning shoot to kill.

These men coming after us are similar to the men I trained with Doc Fullerton and Charlie Platoon down in Rio de Janeiro as a SEAL.

I know exactly what their tactics are. We were in charge of teaching Direct Action Raids as well as hostage recovery to these guys only two years prior to me being here in this old riverboat.

When I was with Charlie Platoon, we did a raid on an island below Pão de Açúcar, the famous mountain with the Jesus statue overlooking Rio.

It was a great mission with the Brazilian SEALs, where we performed a Draeger rebreather dive to the small island, pinned our dive gear under the surface, and then I took a team of lead assault climbers up a cliff to set ropes and assist the rest of the team out of the water and into a house to rescue a simulated hostage.

Because I was a qualified Lead Rock Climbing Instructor for the command I was able to take the team up and lead the route. As a matter of fact, I was wearing the same Israeli desert boots I was wearing now, because of their traction when wet.

The Brazilian SEALs were very professional and solid with their tactics. I shudder at the thought that some of these same guys could be freewheeling justice on the streets out here in the civilian world.

They will be deadly.

With the children tucked in their hiding spots, I lay in the center of the room on my belly, my head facing the door. I keep my hands on the back of my head, and I pray.

"Encante," a voice behind me says.

It is Matheus, and it breaks my heart. The idea of Encante, to escape to the water right now and return to my element, is incredibly tempting. The thought of bringing the children to a safe place with me is indeed enchanting. But here I lay. Real life sucks.

It is in this moment that it hits me; this moment isn't about making a good TV show, or making me out to be some kind of a hero. This is real stakes life-or-death stuff. This is about risking my life to help make a difference, to make life a little better or a little safer for the vulnerable and less fortunate.

Real life is messy, and it is ugly.

My life is about finding the beauty in it, taking the hand of others and guiding them to Encante one day at a time, one evolution at a time. So, here I am.

My best chance tonight with the children is to keep them hidden and let me be the distraction. I make a decision right there to sacrifice myself rather than run for my own preservation or hide like a scared Little Bird.

The risks of my decision are great.

I can be shot on sight.

I can be dragged off to prison and hell on Earth.

Or I can run, get over the side of the boat, and slip into the water.

I lay and I pray as the flashlights shine around the vessel and the noise increases. I think about making sure Doc knows if I get thrown in prison tonight. He will be able to tell Sir Peter and the judge.

The sound of heavy boots and men yelling in Portuguese outside is deafening. I hear the police shout and challenge someone and then hear Roxy speak softly.

She is still on the deck outside.

There are flashlights everywhere and the shapes of men approach the locked wooden doors. Boots, boots, and more boots thud on the planks. The men in black uniforms walk around outside the locked doors and black boots approach the threshold. It is flooded with spotlights.

Do not move, I tell myself. *Stay calm.*

GET UP AND RUN! my inner voice screams.

None of us move.

The door is kicked open.

I hold my breath with Matheus nearby. The others do not make a peep.

The men rush the deck of the boat after what seems ages. They take me away, leaving the children behind, still hidden in the cubbyholes. The Little Birds are safe, but my own personal version of hell begins at this moment.

When I am taken onto the deck of the vessel, Zella is lying in a pool of blood.

The contortions of her facial features were tellingly male, the makeup providing the decorative shell, like an Easter egg, now broken open.

I slip on the grey matter and blood on deck as I am roughly pushed down the gangplank and onto the muddy shore of the Rio Negro.

I get hit on the back of my knees and someone pushes my skull forward, forcing my face down into the mud.

I see stars, but I take pleasure in the soft mud cushioning my face upon impact.

Then the beating starts.

I go into shock when the boots strike my torso. It is a quick volley, but rapidly ceased when an authority figure approaches.

There is a flurry of conversation and a bit of argument, but I am never addressed directly.

The men throw a hood over my head and push me into an awaiting truck. My hands are bound behind my back in cuffs, and I focus on keeping my fingers laced; it helps keep my arms from getting pulled in opposite directions.

I am leaned up against the warm, naked skin of another male, jammed into the back of a modern-day paddywagon. I grimace from the nauseating sweat of the man, tinged with the foul stench of drugs and alcohol. I know this is one of the river pirates sitting next to me.

He says nothing.

I prepare myself for a fight, but nothing comes, only the sound of the truck revving its diesel engine and the bouncing motion of it moving through the city.

In my estimation these are federal officers or soldiers and they are heading for one of the worst prisons in South America, if not the world.

I am fucked.

At the prison, I am immediately separated from the other prisoners and put into a holding tank.

The only thing I perceive outside of my body is first, the completely dehumanizing experience of being stripped of my clothes, inspected, and being put down on my knees, naked, with my hands bound behind my back.

The hood is now off and I am in a bare concrete room. It is a numbing experience being treated like a prisoner of war, about to be executed in a barren room of concrete with nothing more than a drain for the blood.

There is conversation about me, but never directly to me. They are obviously looking at me being an American in the wrong place and the wrong time with a couple of transgender prostitutes.

It does not look good for me.

I am uncuffed and given only my shorts to wear; then I am escorted into a private cell with a concrete slab and an old, ratty, smelly blanket.

I lay on the slab and cover my body and face from view. I know only one thing…if I go into the overcrowded population of this prison, I will be torn apart.

The guards know this as well.

I lay still in the cell with that blanket all night and into the morning. I swelter in the heat of the building and under the blanket, but I keep myself tucked inside, like my own private fort. I am left alone.

Small pleasures.

I sleep.

During the flurry of the morning activity around my cell, the door opens, and, I am set free. No discussion.

Changed.

When I get back to my hotel, I sleep for two days.

I call Doc as soon as I can.

"You idiot," he says over the cellphone.

"What?"

"Never mind, Breeze. I just have no way to share that one with your mom."

"Let's keep this one a secret, Doc."

"Did you call Sir Peter yet?"

"No."

"He knows all about it through me."

"Ughh. What did he say about it?"

"He said 'cone of silence.'"

"Phew."

"What's next, Breeze?"

"Sierra Two is not in Manaus, brother. No mission, no objective—it's too dangerous here."

"Good. I'll call Pete and give him the update. Make sure you check in."

"Will do, Doc."

"Hey, Breeze, what went down on that boat?"

"Tap. Rack. Bang, Doc. That's all I'm going to say."

I spend the next two days searching for Roxy down at the Opera House, with no luck. They never come back.

My consolation is that I know they can survive this environment better than I can. It just breaks my heart to witness such a difficult life they have.

The voice of Matheus whispering "Encante" on the riverboat that night will stay with me for life. Yet I know in my heart that I have to choose my battles wisely.

I eventually get on the phone with my captain back in Buenos Aires, passing on my thoughts of the current route and objectives for the Amazon expedition. I muster the courage to confide in him about the event with the transgenders on the boat. He thinks I am nuts.

"Let's all of us be safe," he tells me. "Find us an objective. Let me know what you find on the journey north up the Rio Negro,

Mr. Lonergan. Let's stay away from anything that may put you or one of the team in jail or worse."

"Aye, Captain."

"I think we should keep this whole event in the cone of silence, Mr. Lonergan," Sir Peter says.

"Aye, Captain."

"Indeed, if you find any stray Little Birds, let me know if we can we do anything. We have the Prime Minister of New Zealand meeting us in Manaus. Focus on the big picture—find our objective."

"Aye, Captain. Sierra-Two out."

The next morning I awake fully intact, walk to Miguel's house, and give him and Katia a big hug. I will stay here for my remaining nights in Manaus. No more adventures, and no more nightmares in this city for me.

I say no more about my actions and my nightmares in Manaus, Brazil…to anyone.

I make a command decision to move ahead with the safety of Miguel and companionship of Katia, and choose my battles wisely. The battle of the undesirables would be the death of me in Manaus, I can feel it in my soul. Worse, I could end up in prison for life.

Watching the older women and kids create a counterculture among the city is educational for me as a lesson in survival. This knowledge will benefit me, and will save many lives in the future.

My experience at this moment in Manaus planted a seed in my brain to play some part in protecting the children I encounter who are caught in the crossfire of crime and violence.

These Little Birds will affect my decisions in times of war when my odyssey lands on the streets of Baghdad, Iraq, in the not so distant future.

For now, I am glad I am not caught up in the whirlwind of crime in this jungle city; a city filled with demons.

I move farther to the north with Miguel and Katia to find my objective—a place on the map where I can make a difference in this world, and survive. It is not here in Manaus. The last 1,500 miles for me to scout begins at the Venezuelan border.

PHOTO GALLERY

Marc at BUD/S

Marc (R) at BUD/S post Hell Week with
swim buddy Jerry 'Gus' W.

5 Knots BUD/S (photo: US Navy)

BUD/S 207 LPO Andy N.

Doc Fullerton (left)

Marc training South American Special Forces

Sir Peter Blake

Seamaster on the ice shelf at 70 South

Kiting the motored paraglider on the
ice shelf with Abbo and Janot

Lift off—paraglider flight at 70 South

Marc under the ice at 70 South looking
out to the stern of *Seamaster*

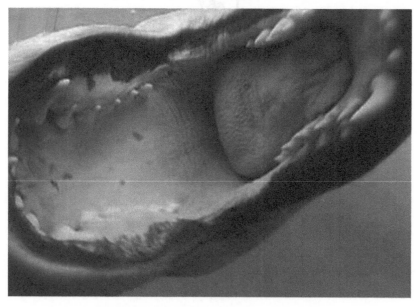

Actual Leopard Seal frame grab from the
underwater camera under the ice at 70 South

Seamaster enroute north two days before
man overboard (Marc is on the bow)

Miguel and his captain One-Eyed Jack
beaching *Iguana* on Dolphin Island

Marc scouting Sierra Two (photo D. Weniger)

Scouting Iguana River to Sierra Two (photo D. Weniger)

Eating a meal with Luis before the death of my guide (D. Weniger)

Basi and Marc scouting Sierra Two (D. Weniger)

Departing our first encounter with Hoti (photo D. Weniger)

Blakexpeditions Jungle Team (Marc in wide brimmed hat)

Seamaster II heading to Mt. Aracamoni

Jungle Camp Sierra Two

Jungle Team aboard *Seamaster*
(from left Abbo, Marc, Janot, Ollie)

Janot on the bow of *Seamaster* enroute to the Amazon

Marc after the news of Sir Peter's death

Marc enroute east to Iraq

Marc in Iraq during Operation Guardian Angel

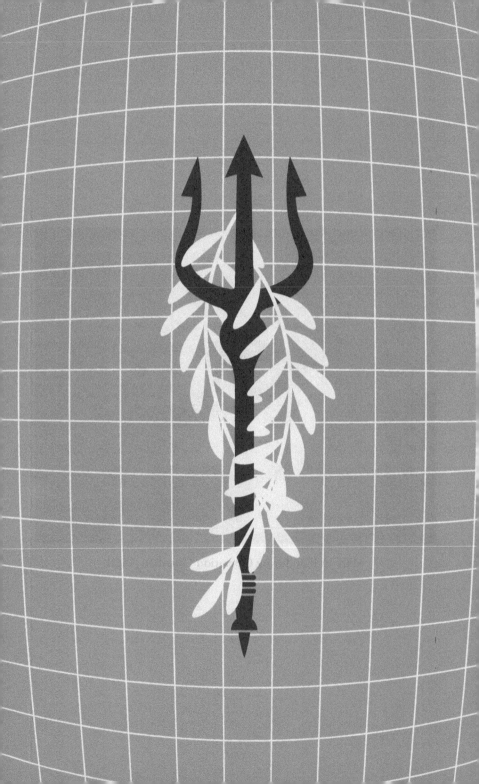

VENEZUELA

Colombia—Venezuela—Brazil Border
Cucuí, Brazil
SPRING 2001
AUTHOR AGE: 34

When I land in Cucuí, I am definitely in an Amazonian border town. After abandoning the Cessna and fist bumping the pilot, I gather all my belongings.

My number one rule for travel is I can only take that which I can carry for miles if I have to. That means it slings over my shoulder, or, like my Pelican Case, is carried like a briefcase. No wheeled bags, no bulky cases. Over my shoulder I place the right pack strap of my NorthFace mountaineering backpack. It has been my companion since I got off of the boat, from the Roosevelt to the Rio Negro to now.

In my hands are my two Pelican cases. I am hopeful all goes as planned up here. I am extremely vulnerable right now.

A man approaches me near the docks of Cucuí. "Are you here to see the Yanomami?" He has a slightly European accent.

"Si, *Jefe*."

"You are Marco, si?" He dips his head.

"Si, *Jefe*, I'm Marco. Doc told me you would be here."

"There are two men in a large dugout canoe down on the river. Go to them." The man gestures down to a wharf about a hundred yards below our position. "Find the fair skinned guy down there with a shaved head. He is Dante. He will be your guide."

"Can I trust him?"

"Don't trust anyone on the rivers."

"Roger that, *Jefe*. Thanks for meeting me here."

"Don't talk to any boat with a Colombian flag painted on it. You will never be seen again. These are bad people."

"Entiendo Jefe. Gracias." I understand, thank you.

The mysterious man walks up the river and boards a speedboat waiting for him. There is a calm coxswain at the helm. The vessel has no markings or flag. The boat speeds north. I am not sure who the man is, but he is definitely connected with either a Venezuelan or a Colombian Special Forces unit. I think the latter.

Doc had given me specific instructions to stay clear of Colombia at all costs, even just forays into small towns on the Orinoco River up ahead.

I make my way down a white sand beach and navigate over some smooth rocks until I can make out a beat-up dugout canoe with two men laboring over an old outboard motor.

One man has a shaved head and is a lighter complexion than many of the local Indios working the river bank community dock.

I walk to him, scanning for Colombian flags anywhere on the vessel. None found. I walk close enough to announce myself.

"Lucho, hand me a plug wrench!" the man barks. He is aware of my approach but shouts the command as if it goes right through me and over to his first mate.

The man glances at me briefly. His dark facial hair is shaved to a goatee. His brown eyes spark but quickly go back to his outboard motor on the back of the canoe.

The entire deck inside the vessel, approximately twenty feet in length, is cluttered. Fuel cans, food wrappers, empty water bottles, various machetes, and a shotgun with a basic sling made out of the sinew of some form of vegetation. Several wet and soggy maps are on the makeshift seats that might be fuel containers. There is also an old HF radio tucked up into the bow of the canoe with a battery pack and an old canvas bag, out of which is sticking a long wire antenna.

I pick up on it quick.

As a SEAL sniper, I was dependent on my skills with HF radios to communicate through the dense jungles and back to base, back to my platoon chief, Doc Fullerton. My life depended on being able to talk with Doc, so I learned everything from sat comms to VHF line of sight radios like the ones we used in Honduras following Hurricane Mitch.

The radio in the front of the boat was a Vietnam era radio with hand-crank battery power capability.

I check out Dante's motor as he labors away. It is clean and obviously well maintained. A good sign.

From the back, I can see he has the same taste in outdoor clothing as myself. He is wearing a lightweight shirt designed for fly fishermen, like the one I am currently wearing. The dirt-stained button-down is brown, but was obviously once white. On his feet are a pair of high top leather snake boots, like many of the Cabocles wear in the jungle. He is wearing a dark ball cap and lightweight cargo-style pants like me. I like this guy already.

That is when he hits me in the stomach with the back side of his hand without even a glance at me.

"Hey!"

"If you're going to stand there and gawk, hand me that wrench from Lucho."

Without me noticing, Lucho had come up directly behind me. The dark-skinned Venezuelan puts a socket wrench in my hand and turns away to speak to a Yanomami teenage boy in his native tongue.

"Wrench!" I hand it to Dante. "Move around me and cycle the motor!" he orders.

I move to the front of the outboard and locate the handle on the starting pull cord. "Ready."

"Go ahead."

I pull the starter and let him screw around with the plug and the single two-stroke cylinder. He screws the plug in and checks the arc of the spark to its white ceramic crown.

"Pop off the air filter and give it a go."

I locate the filter, pop it off, and fire up the motor.

It starts with one pull.

"Beginner's luck!" he says over the tinny roar of the 40 horsepower motor.

Coughing, I choke from the rush of smoke from the excess oil in the motor being burned off. It stings my lungs and eyes.

The man laughs. He extends his right hand and shakes mine with an iron grip. "I am Dante. Where are you going?"

"I'm Marc. I'm trying to get into Venezuela and chart an expedition path."

"What path? Are you looking for Yanomami?"

"I'm following Cousteau's floatplane scout up through the Casiquiari, hoping to do some work. I hear a lot about the Yanomami."

"You're the American, ya?"

"Yeah, I'm the scout for the international film project."

"Cool. You met Lucho?"

He nods to my back and Lucho is right behind my shoulder again.

"You're a wily one," I say to him.

He has big brown eyes and an even bigger smile, a wavy mat of dark hair on his head, and a lean build. Lucho is wearing a pair of faded blue athletic shorts and no shoes or sandals.

"Soy Lucho, chamo."

"Chamo! It's been a while since I heard that word," I reply in Spanish.

Dante grins. "Welcome to the Lost World, Marco."

"Yeah, well, that's my objective. The Lost World."

"I am pretty much the only one in the region that can help you with that and actually succeed." My new guide gestures to the distant mountain ranges to the north of us. "It's a long and dangerous journey from here."

"I know, Dante. I do need to tell the natural story of the region but would love to dig in with the Indios."

Two teenaged Yanomami boys are shuttling gear for Lucho. The boys appear to be twins and have distinctive facial features with large, friendly eyes, although they have an unusual distant stare, slightly detached.

"You will fly with me back to our base camp in Puerto Ayacucho. I will show you where you need to go with Sir Peter Blake, Marco."

Dante leaves Lucho and the team back at the dugout; the "bongo" as they call it. He and the Yanomami boys will begin the preparations of acquiring another matching dugout to prep for the expedition run.

Today we have a beautiful, clear, crisp sky. We bump gently over the top of the Amazon in a Cessna 206. Below, a snakelike river is winding its way in the same trajectory as our flight.

It seems everything is leading us to the base of the looming flattop mountains to our north.

"Marco, there are several *tepuis* we can explore here in Venezuela. Neblina to the south. Aracamoni is south central, La Esmeralda north central, and Sierra Magualida is north.

"These mountain ranges form the Guiana Shield, not like a single wall but like towers guarding the Amazonas. If we focus your journey on any of these *tepuis*, we focus on any of the many tribes of the Lost World. These lost tribes do still exist, you just have to be willing and able to boat long distances and to hike into *la selva*."

After about an hour's flight, Dante points below us as we fly over a large, expansive valley in the mountain range. We fly into the open end of a horseshoe shaped mountain and follow a large whitewater river up its center, which climbs in altitude towards the summit of the mountain.

"Down below is a sacred *tepui*, Marco. A sacred mountain to the Yanomami. To access any of the *tepuis* that I talk about, we must take a bongo up the whitewater rapids we encounter on the climb to the heart of the mountain range." It is tricky and it is dangerous. "That's the boat we have in Cucuí. We just finished a river trip in this area. The film crew got scared and we doubled back. It was a waste of our time."

"Yeah, the boat was a mess, Dante."

"We have only a few intrepid souls that come out here, mostly to Neblina." Indicating a tributary of the whitewater river that makes a steep climb, Dante says, "This is where we were heading. No one comes here as a tourist."

"What's down there?" I ask, my head spinning from near vertigo looking down into the depth of the prehistoric land below.

"Aracamoni—your objective for the expedition," my guide answers. "There is an illegal gold mine below us, killing the indigenous people and destroying a sacred rain forest. This mountain is the holy place of the Yanomami."

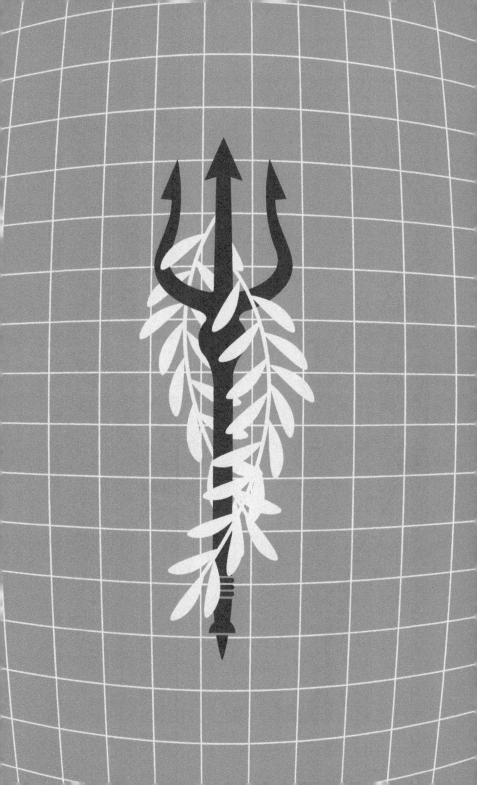

Puerto Ayacucho

Guardia Nacional

Coromoto

Cucui'

Gold Mine

Sierra Two

Dante

PUERTO AYACUCHO

Gateway to Amazonas, Venezuela
SPRING 2001
AUTHOR AGE: 34

The next morning I wake up in the guest bedroom of Dante's villa.

We are on the outskirts of a bustling jungle town referred to as the gateway to the Venezuelan Amazon. My guide invited me to stay in his house while we work out the logistics to continue our trek.

Dante is spun up with excitement over our future endeavors, but I find it curious as he is so cryptic about our objective. It is as if he is keeping it close to his chest, so I do not shoot it down. This objective to find an illegal gold mine is obviously important to him. The one thing I have learned in my endeavors with subject matter experts is that, if they are passionate about something we are doing, we should let it roll.

My new friend's house is made from concrete blocks and painted light pink on the interior walls of the room I slept in overnight. The bed is a comfortable four-poster with a mosi-net draped over its tall frame. A ceiling fan above churns away in cadence with a slight breeze outside. The air is warm and humid, but comfortable. I roll out of bed wearing a loose pair of black Calvin Klein underwear, my official sleeping outfit since I arrived in the Amazon Basin in Brazil. I cover myself in baby powder before I hit the ham-

mock or the bed at night. In these warm climates it helps absorb
sweat and keeps my linens clean.

The slab of the clean concrete floor is cool and refreshing to
my bare feet. I walk toward the sound of kids playing outside my
bedroom window. It is 7 am.

I open a pair of wooden slat shutters that double for windows
and look out to an open courtyard. Dante's wife is out in the center
playing with her two young daughters. The trio is being enter-
tained by a kitten.

There is a grumpy-looking old man walking in their periph-
ery pretending to be disinterested in them, but I notice his regular glances to the playful banter livening the mood of the
gated compound.

All three of the ladies outside are surprisingly blonde haired
with fair complexions.

A knock comes on the door behind me.

"Marco, are you up?"

"Yeah, come on in."

Dante enters my room wearing only a pair of cotton boxers and
a ball cap. He has the same body frame as me, but with dark hair.
It's a funny picture to me.

"I see we dress alike even outside of the jungle, Dante."

"A man's home is his castle, Marco."

"It's a beautiful home, my friend."

"*Tranquilo, chamo.*"

"You have a beautiful family as well. Who's the old man?"

"That's my father-in-law. We call him *El Govierno*. The
Governor. He used to be the governor of the region. He lost his
wife not long ago and lives in a cottage on the other side of the
property." Dante points across the gardens and palm trees to a par-
cel of walled land.

"He still considers himself important, so my wife and her sisters keep him out in his own corner of the property so he can rule over himself and his little piece of land."

"Sounds lonely."

"Yes, but he has his way of participating, doesn't he?"

"You look like you have it dialed in well, Dante. Nice set-up!"

"I try. It's a lot of work. My maid will do your laundry and bring you a change of clothes for breakfast. We'll eat, then head into the office in town and go over maps."

"Sounds good, amigo."

At that, Dante's wife frames herself in the open shutters of the window, rests her arms on the lower part of the frame, and leans in. "I see you two explorers are dressed and ready for the jungle." The blonde-haired woman is attractive and athletic in stature. She looks to be in her mid-thirties like me and Dante.

"Marco, this is Lena, my wife."

"*Un placer*, Lena," I say with a gesture of respect and a slight bow.

"*Placer*, Marco. You look after my man up there. I hear you are going up to the Hoti lands, *es la verdad?*"

"*Si, Mamacita,*" Dante responds. "*La verdad.*"

"Marco, you give him a hand up there," she tells me. "He tries to do too much sometimes!"

"*Si*, Lena, *entiendo*."

After a meal of fried bananas and pancakes, Dante and I drive into Puerto Ayacucho in his 1984 Jeep CJ-7 Laredo.

He has the top open, except for a faded black bikini top, no doors, and the windshield folded down.

The wind blows directly in our faces as he dodges stray dogs and honking four-by-four trucks through the busy streets.

PA, as they call it, is a typical adventure gateway city in my observation, housing the usual internet cafes and coffee shops, outdoor equipment stores, and various government buildings. There is a large pizza restaurant, obviously the town's party hub.

"Karaoke tonight, *chamo*, if you are up for a beer later!"

"You're on!"

"We have many miles to cover by river and by land. We need to enjoy this time while we have it!" Dante shouts over the rush of wind.

He screeches to a halt in front of a building with a large wooden carved placard reading Aventuras Amazonas. "This is base camp. You want a coffee, Marco?"

"Yeah!"

"Get settled in and start over the maps with Manny inside, I'll be right back."

Dante bolts into a cafe and into the company of several local men, obviously greeting him with various requests and niceties.

Dante seems to be the mayor of this town. He definitely looks to be the best guide I can ask for in this neck of the woods.

Inside the office, I am greeted by walls plastered in large maps of the surrounding jungle. The place smells like adventure.

Sandalwood incense burns in the corner and the scent of musty canvas and waterproof gear bags permeate the large concrete-walled office. There is a single desk with a large brown surface, apparently to aid in the reading of large maps.

Off to the side is a corner desk with a large wooden carving depicting two bottle-nosed dolphins swimming in synchronous twirls.

"Hey man!"

I turn around to see a wide-faced teenager with a huge toothy grin facing me.

"My name is Manny. Dante told me about you!" He reminds me of a Venezuelan version of Howdy Doody.

"Hey, Manny. I'm Marco. I need to get a lay of the land, can you help me?"

"Hell yeah, Marco. You know you got the best guide in the country for what you want to do."

"Yeah? What did you hear?"

"You're going after El Tigre!"

"Who's that?" I ask, somewhat dumbfounded.

"Dante has a guide for you. They call him El Tigre de Aracamoni."

"The Tiger?"

"He's the tiger of the mountain. The place he will lead you is Mt. Aracamoni."

I remember the waterfall and the flat top mountain Dante showed me, obviously Mt. Aracamoni.

"Dante called me on the radio from the house," Manny says, nodding to a large military style radio set sitting on a wooden plank. "We run HF here, and I man the fort. Sometimes all we can depend on is each other."

"Do you guys have any backup plan in the bush?"

"We have the Guardia Nacional as a backup. They have helicopters for medevacs, but it is difficult to be dependable."

"Never dependable," I tell him.

"Yeah, Marco, just limited. Many times they just don't have the fuel to move around."

Manny reaches up and takes a large map down from the wall by taking out the thumbnails on each corner. It is a map of the entire Amazon Basin, in excellent condition.

I do not know it at the time, but this will be my only map for the remainder of my adventure in the Amazon. This map will cover over three thousand miles of my journey, and act as a guiding light for me in my darkest times, yet to come.

"Marco, got you a strong coffee. Black. You need sugar?" Dante enters the front door of the adventure outpost. He hits the power button on a stereo in the corner and activates a CD player.

A musical instrument called a flauta plays an engaging South American-flavored tune.

The flauta is like the mythical flute played by Pan, consisting of several reeds lashed together side by side, similar in design to and played like a harmonica. It has an aboriginal tone and texture to its melodic notes as it dances in an upbeat cadence to drums and various stringed instruments on the background of the piece.

"Straight up, *chamo*, thank you."

Dante hands me a warm porcelain coffee mug and I cradle it in my hands while my guide takes control of the map table, picks up a sharpened pencil, and starts pointing. I like what I see in his actions.

As I have learned from Sir Peter Blake in our expedition to Patagonia and below, a true navigator uses an implement, not a digit. Two points for the house of Dante.

He traces the area we had recently flown over. "Traveling into this area is dangerous and it is remote, even by our standards." Dante glances at Manny and gives his helper a knowing look that I cannot interpret. "Our logistics base camp is a town called Manapiare. It is a settlement that balances on the edge of mountain ranges to the north and to the east."

"What is the range to the north?" I ask, pointing to a large cluster of mountains with the distinct horseshoe shape I had seen to be indicative of the Guiana Shield. Another mountain range rising above the steamy jungle and into the cool air of the higher elevations, it is another *tepui*.

"This is Majagua. I have been working with some researchers studying Hoti Indians in this region. There are many semi-nomadic bands of these Indios in this region. We call them the naked ones. We are going into the Sierra Magualida...over here to the east." Dante moves his pointer to a large cluster of contour lines. The large mountain range we flew over yesterday.

I recognize the shapes on the map and my eyes follow the twisting shapes of various rivers in the deep cuts surrounding the 3,000-foot granite peak.

"What's up there?" I ask, drawing an imaginary circle around the area of the map, gauging the spatial parameters of the geographic area he is focusing on.

"By the way, how do we set up my billing?" Dante asks.

"I'll email back to *Seamaster* today, once we agree on a plan, and start to brief my captain. I will put you in touch directly with Sir Peter while we continue our planning and hopefully execution."

"Good. Back to the map. Our journey will be an expedition from the town of Manapiare, here, aboard a large bongo piloted by my river captain for the region. Alberto will take us down the Ventuari River, here." Dante traces a large river south from a small town on the map and runs it roughly thirty miles east through a flat valley. "We will pass the Majagua region and continue to the Asita River." He finds the fork in the river and traces the squiggly line of the Asita north in a twisting path toward a large sloping valley about twelve miles from the fork, as the crow flies. "We will make our way north for a day and camp in this Protestant mission at the base of Magaulida."

"Appears easy enough," I say. "We can get nature shots along the way. I'll use it in a presentation for Sir Peter and the gang to showcase what we will see up here in the Venezuelan leg of the expedition. Our objective is to find El Tigre, right?"

"Oh, yeah."

"Where do we go from the missionary base?"

"Leave that to me," answers my guide.

"It all starts with a trip up the Parásito River with two of my guides, it is a quick journey with less mountains, good to get production photos for your captain...and to practice."

"Doesn't that mean 'parasite,' Dante?"

"Yes."

I am going to need a good traveller/photographer on this one.

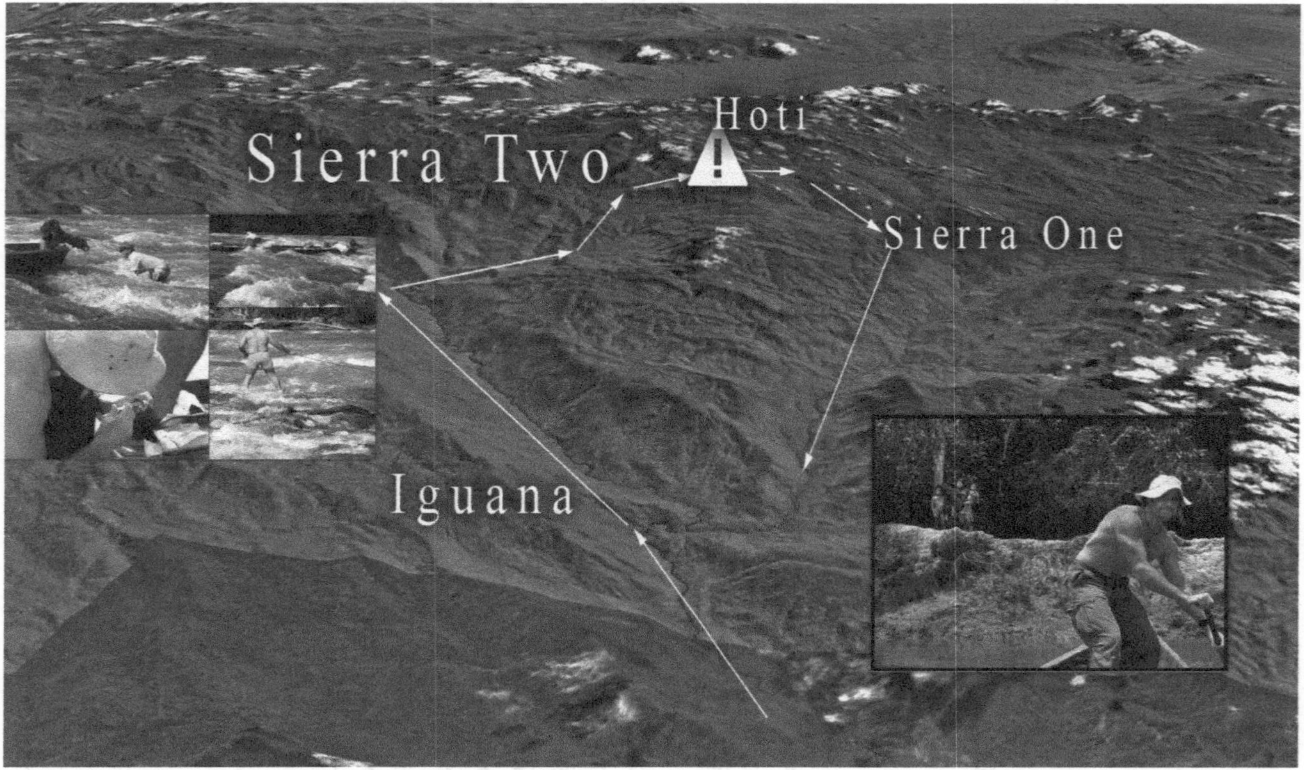
Sierra Two
Hoti
Sierra One
Iguana

SIERRA TWO: RIVER OF DEATH

Sierra Magualida, Venezuela
SUMMER 2001
AUTHOR AGE: 34

I invited a close friend and professional photographer named Dana to join me on the first journey into the Tepuis so we could build a slideshow of river travel and a packing list for Nat Geo and for Sir Peter and the crew. It was a ten day journey without Dante, but I got to work with two of his guides and achieve an important mission with Dana.

I got a taste of what is ahead on Sierra Two, in steeper mountainous terrain, and it opened my eyes.

After regrouping with Dante later, and flying our gear out from Puerto Ayacucho again, the team makes it upriver from Manapiare without incident and is on the beach near a Protestant mission below Sierra Magualida. We are in place to reach our objective—the river I call Sierra Two. We will begin ascending a narrow canyon filled with a tumbling whitewater river.

Luis has started a fire and prepares a meal of piranha that he caught earlier with Alberto. Around the campfire, I make my assessment of the cast of characters.

Dante is our team leader. He has years of experience in the regions of Venezuela and works with many, if not all the indigenous tribes. He has proven himself to be trustworthy and professional, and will easily skirt the edges for a bit of fun.

Case in point, he proudly offered to bury me on a hill with a good view if I die on this expedition. It sounds brutal, but up here in the wilderness help is days away. The cold reality is you live or die here. Death simply means returning to the cycle of growth in the jungle, nothing more.

Dante is dressed like me, in poplin cargo pants and a white lightweight button-down shirt. He's wearing the dark blue Blakexpeditions ball cap I gave him earlier. His face is clean-shaven except for a goatee and he has a red bandana tied around his neck like a proper swashbuckler. His tan leather belt has a leather sheath that holds a knife his wife gave him as a gift. The knife has a curved blade at the tip designed to cut through rope or line easily.

In the parachuting world, we call this type of blade a hook knife. I keep mine on my chest strap of my Vector parachute pack. If I become entangled by paracord I can pull the hooked blade out of its sheath and slice cord effortlessly.

I know Dante's world revolves around moving heavy wooden canoes up and down cascading whitewater rivers. The big rivers have the most civilized experiences only a tourist would appreciate. The real deal is up and down the whitewater rivers. You simply have to earn it back here.

"The reward is equal to the effort," Doc would tell me. I agree. Dante has lightweight canvas boots like mine as well. I can tell he is most interested in the water part of this journey and does not consider himself to be much of a hiker. He is going to try to access as much as he can on the rivers. The timing is good since the rainy season is beginning.

Alberto is wearing a dirty pair of dress slacks, a dirty button-down dress shirt, and a pair of high top leather snake boots. Slung over his shoulder is a Winchester 12 gauge shotgun that seems a part of his anatomy. He is also wearing a Blakexpeditions ball cap over his scruffy black hair. He has large, bright eyes and a bigger smile.

I have learned to watch for the moments he loses the smile, either on the water or in the jungle. This is when I have my guard up the most.

I already have a bit of experience with Alberto, not only in the boat and on this particular river, but also hiking, hunting, and gathering with him deep inland. Alberto is an excellent hiker.

Luis is stoking the fire. He is half naked and overweight. The heaviest of the group. He reminds me of Fred Flintstone with the beard and the big neck. Luis has friendly eyes but does not smile as much as the other guys. He is wearing a pair of plastic flip-flops on his feet and a pair of orange bicycle shorts. He has a floppy white hat I gave him from the earlier trip, which is now dirty and not well taken care of.

Luis has shown me some of the same tendencies I saw long ago in my military experience with less than ideal teammates, before my days as a SEAL. On my earlier trip with him, I would notice little things, like him serving himself more food than he needed, or being disrespectful. Although he called himself Dante's naturalist, he did not contribute much to my experience understanding nature in the region. I did like to fish with him though.

Luis, Alberto, and I can catch some piranha, I tell you.

I am good at catching the fruit eating variety, but Luis and Alberto know how to find and catch the meat eaters. The Caribe. Those are the tasty ones!

Luis has our one steel pot braced over the fire to heat water for coffee. The water is boiling and I roll into the ship's supplies on the bongo. We have one large plastic drum that holds our food supplies. Basics—coffee, which I find right away. There is also plenty of rice and beans, some fresh water bottles, soup stock, and some fresh fruit. No booze.

Dante runs a tight ship and does not like it when Luis or Alberto get into the drink. The captain made a point to keep things safe and return to his wife and daughters after all these years in the jungle.

Of all the guides in Amazonas, Dante is the one to take you the deepest and darkest. Like me, he only takes what he considers acceptable risks.

In the front of the bongo are all our backpacks. Alberto has an old suitcase full of who knows what. Luis has a backpack and a plastic garbage bag full of personal stuff. Dante and I have vinyl waterproof backpacks designed for kayakers.

My yellow bag has a Blakexpeditions sticker on it. It's the same bag I wore on my back when flying over Antarctica and Patagonia. If I hit the water back then, I had a survival suit and a waterproof pack with the basics to survive. The pack is perfect for the Amazon.

Under our backpacks is the ship's radio. It is similar to the one Dante had with Lucho down in Cucuí. It is a long wire HF radio with VHF capability. It looks like it belongs in a Vietnam-era war movie, like *Apocalypse Now* or something.

In jungle missions with Doc Fullerton, he and I would work long-range jungle communications all the time. I am accustomed to going out into the bush and radioing back to him at base camp.

I worked the same communications plan with Manny the first time I came out here. I know how to use it and call for help. At least, get word back to Manny. Or at worst, have Manny email Sir Peter from the office in Puerto Ayacucho down to *Seamaster* in Buenos Aires. An absolute worst case scenario is to contact Doc via email back at SEAL Team Four Headquarters.

I think that communicating with Doc is more of a buddy looking out for me, as he has done helping me plan. What I do not understand at this time is that Sir Peter and Doc Fullerton have a secret pact, a promise by Doc to safeguard me at any cost that he can muster working back at SEAL Team Four Headquarters.

He told Sir Peter, "If Marco gets in trouble, he will have a team of SEALs on the deck and pulling him out if that is needed."

I have a Guardian Angel back at command headquarters, even out here in the most remote regions as a civilian explorer.

Had I known about this pact at this particular moment of my odyssey I would not have freewheeled this expedition so much with Dante. I could have done a better job with an op order on the mission to find Tigre.

I did not build any contingencies with Doc or any drop dead times to check in with him and Sir Peter. I am truly on my own up here from this point on.

Big mistake.

Returning to the boiling water with the coffee and an old beat-up coffee pot, I make a brew of cowboy coffee—simply pouring the ground coffee into the boiling water.

We drink the coffee and let our teeth filter the grounds and spit them onto the sand at our feet as we chat. After breakfast we push upriver. I stay amidships with Luis while Dante navigates the rocks and small rapids from the bow.

Alberto manages the outboard motor from behind. It is your typical outboard you see in the developed world. The top end looks like an exposed lawnmower motor with a straight vertical shaft about four feet long that sticks out below the wooden hull of the bongo. At the end is a beat-up propeller. It is a heavy motor, inefficient to move up and down the rivers, and it is dangerous. Alberto is a pro and handles the motor with ease.

We have twenty miles to navigate and they are all uphill. We begin in an open valley with the knife-edge mountain range to our west, the Sierra Magualida looming over our right shoulders to the east, and the climbing valley of the Iguana River to our north.

Today our objective is a set of headwaters only five miles up the river, but it will take us the rest of the afternoon to make it. I have done the route before to the headwaters with Alberto so I know what we are in for.

The water level on this run is slightly higher, which gives us a little more current to deal with. Three miles upriver, we reach our first set of rapids.

Dante points out the whitewater ten meters ahead and the three of us exit the boat. I am the first one out on the starboard side, Luis on the port side. Dante moves along the outside of the boat toward me. Alberto moves up alongside Luis after he secures the silenced motor and vertical shaft with a rubber bungee cord to keep the prop sticking high out of the water.

The rubber soles of my desert boots grip large, slippery boulders roughly the size of human skulls. The cool river water saturates my long pants up to my waist as I step upstream into dramatically shallow water. The current is extremely strong, running down from the mountain valley ahead. The whitecaps dance like a herd of wild horses stampeding toward us in a rush to escape what lies above.

I grab the boat with my hands and feel the warm, slippery texture of the hollowed out tree canoe. It looks and feels like a massive crocodile, the scarred, rough surface like the scales of a reptile. Its incredible weight is cumbersome and almost intimidating in the strong current.

I make a point of never putting myself downstream of the 30-foot beast in case she gets loose and turns sideways over me.

I try to have two solid points of contact whenever I stop walking so I can push the boat forward. I stay off to her side.

Dante leads the way through the rapids and our team moves the boat farther and farther until we are past the challenging shallows.

Alberto enters the boat and powers up the motor by wrapping the start cord around its cap and pulling quickly. The motor sputters to life and he releases the bungee, dropping the prop into the bubbling waters of Sierra Magualida.

Dante jumps into the bow while Luis and I hold the boat in the middle. Dante was already in neck deep water and barely got himself over the edge of the boat with a slight jump off the rocky bottom.

Luis pushes himself inside the boat prematurely and forces the vessel off course toward me. It starts the boat moving sideways across the current over the top of me as the swell of water takes control of the port side of the boat. I hold on to starboard and plant my feet firmly on the boulders.

Alberto guns the motor and the eggbeater prop churns the water far to stern, hooking the boat to the left and upstream. The stern sweeps toward me and I lose my grip on the crocodile for a moment. With the churning propeller arcing in towards me I grab the side of the boat and hoist myself in.

I give Luis a death stare as I get settled into place and Alberto continues our trek to the north. Luis is completely oblivious to my ire.

"Luis, cuidado cuando regresando la barca!" I explain sternly.

He replies in rapid Spanish that goes beyond my ability to process but generally means something about the water being higher and faster.

"No shit, Luis," I say in English. *"La próxima vez que esté en el lado corriente abajo del barco, entiendo?"* Next time get in on the upriver side, idiot.

"Si, *chamo*," he responds politely.

Luis is a good guy, I just can't trust him with my safety.

I already pegged Alberto as being a good SEAL type of operator. He is a strong, silent professional. His lithe, muscular build always seems in the right place at the right time in awkward situations. He is an expert at what he specializes in: running a motor and steering our boat up through treacherous rapids. He would definitely be an excellent candidate for the Special Boats (SWCC) SEAL boat operators.

As a Piaroa Indian who has grown up on these rivers, this man is in his element, and I respect that.

Dante on the bow reminds me of an Army Special Forces guy. He works, speaks, and lives with native indigenous cultures and adapts to their ways to accomplish complex missions that do not exploit them to the point they lose base with their culture and beliefs. He doesn't try to change them or manipulate them. He simply finds the best way to work with them, make a buck as a guide, and come home safely to his beautiful wife and kids.

He is also awkward in the water. He is not the best swimmer in the group, and I laughed watching him mount the boat back at the rapids. He was goofy getting back in, but he made it all the same.

I notice Luis's leg is bleeding, right above his ankle. It is a pin-sized hole of red blood streaming out and into the bottom of the boat. Luis is unaware of the wound.

THE WARNING

Sierra Two River, Amazonas
SUMMER 2001
AUTHOR AGE: 34

"Luis! Que hacen?" I ask.

He glances down and shrugs, then in a moment, starts wincing and writhing in agony.

I start laughing, because he is only in pain *after* he sees the wound.

"Ahhhhhhh!" he shrieks and grabs his ankle.

"Fue mordido por una raya!" Alberto says of the commotion.

"In English, Beto," I request.

"Bit by a stingray!" he shouts over the motor.

I move up to the bow next to Dante and uncover my waterproof pack. I pull out my black full-sized medical pack and take out a blue nylon medical kit that Doc gave me back in the States.

In the smaller med kit I have irrigating syringes and a container of saline solution. The syringe has a long, flexible needle to stick into wounds and flush them out.

I clean the wound, pour some iodine on it, dry it, then put some crazy glue over the top to seal it off and keep it waterproof.

These poisonous rays are in the rocks up here. It's crazy! These are the same stingrays I see in the sandy shallows of the Pacific Ocean when I surf out at Blacks Beach in San Diego. They are the same size and carry the same powerful venom that makes wherever they touch feel like someone has taken a sledgehammer and whacked you. It is *sooo* painful.

I did learn to keep the injured part of your body under the water or buried in the sand. The venom reacts violently to oxygen.

I also learned that you can pee on it to ease the pain, but that doctor ain't in town for Luis.

We navigate to the next set of rapids. We have only moved up about three hundred yards.

Dante exits the bow and Alberto secures the motor. I get out of the boat and gently push Luis off to the downstream side. We push the boat through the rapid section and return to our positions in the crocodile.

As we get settled back into place, I watch up the canyon as we wind deeper and deeper into what is called The Lost World. We pass a village on the eastern bank of the Iguana River and Alberto waves to a group of women and children doing laundry and bathing in the river.

These are Enepa Indians. The Enepa are primarily from the eastern and southern regions. Alberto's tribe, Piaroa, are from a Caribe sect to the north and west closer to the Caribbean.

Although both tribes speak separate languages, they are similar in appearance and cultural aspects. They are markedly different from the third tribe in the region, the Hoti.

We encountered small bands of semi-civilized tribes along the mountain river. I stay close to Alberto and listen to him communicate in many dialects with the various tribes. He reminds me of local assets we would utilize for our missions in the jungles across the continent for our SEAL missions, particularly the guides we would utilize to work on sniper set missions.

I check on Luis and see he has another wound, right above his last one. This one is much larger, and a bigger bleed.

"Luis, *tu pierna!*" I gesture to his leg.

He moans. "Ahhhhhhh!"

I move to repeat the medical drill and bump my right ankle on the boat. *OUCH!* I pull up my pant leg and I'll be darned. I have the same type of wound, right over the top of my canvas boot on my right calf.

"Fuck."

Big mistake. The air hits my bloody mark and the pain starts. The puncture wound is a big mamma. I can just about put my finger in it.

We are barely into this journey and I am already burning through my saline and crazy glue.

I rub some Neosporin onto Luis's wound and dress my own. This is going to be a long day.

Five miles upriver and ten more portages later we are a wreck.

Dante wisely follows Alberto's lead and puts on his snake boots. I do the opposite by peeling off my cargo pants and putting on a pair of surfing shorts; I keep my canvas boots on since I do not have any snake boots to wear. Now I know why these guys wear these boots on the water.

We make camp for the night as the sun is starting to drift below the knife ridge mountain to our west. I nickname the mountain range K-Bar Ridge. It towers over us in a daunting fashion. It is much more ominous than the mass of Sierra Magaulida to our east.

The Sierra appears to be a habitable zone of lush mountain jungles, rivers, and waterfalls. It is truly like a Garden of Eden.

K-Bar Ridge to the east looks like it belongs to King Kong. I am not eager to climb those steep ridges into the cloudy weather top of the range. I am grateful we are going to be heading east the next day.

Alberto and Luis go off to fish up a quiet tributary and leave Dante and me at camp. He and I set up our hammocks and the mosi nets. We also tie up tarps over the hammocks to prepare for the oncoming deluge of rain that has been building all day.

It is springtime here and not rainy season, but when the weather does sink into this Amazonian valley and trap itself up against the Guiana Shield, it rains mercilessly.

So far the worst things have been the rays and the mosquitoes that come out at this time of the day. It has been relatively dry and they are not too bad up to this part of the river. I do not trust the fish and the snakes in the waters up here. There is also the risk of the Candiru fish that will swim up your urethra and lodge itself in your bladder with hooklike gills.

Uggghhhh.

Never pee underwater is the rule. That is what opens the gate to the tiny snakelike fish swimming into your body.

I move to the sandy edge of the river with a large plastic bucket wearing only my surf shorts. I dip the bucket in the river and pour its contents over my head. I take out a bar of soap from my hygiene kit and scrub my body. This is a routine I have made a part of my life since I entered Venezuela.

So far I have spent over three months in the Amazon on my own, and I have a lot to show for it.

I just have to find El Tigre to make the journey a complete mission, then focus with Dante on the logistics of the Venezuela leg of the expedition.

We are running a bit low on protein for our meals since we have not had time to hunt or fish.

I cook up a pot of rice over our campfire and scrounge for something to add to it while it cools. When I return toward the fire, I catch Luis eating the entire pot of rice. I stop for a moment and watch him from the forest. He does not know I see him, and my heart sinks. I have seen this behavior before. I better keep an eye on this guy; he cannot be trusted.

Squatting on the sand in the cooling jungle air, I spot a few capybara swimming across the river from the opposite bank and

I lose my train of thought. I sit still and watch the giant creatures bob across the one hundred or so meters of water from the far bank over to mine. Quite curious beasts they are. They look like the world's largest chipmunks. According to the locals, they are quite the delicacy.

When they reach my side of the river, I hear Alberto's shotgun and then the thud of one of the beasts hitting the ground and thrashing a bit.

Beto brings the massive rodent to the camp and guts it, cleans it, pulls the back strap off its carcass, and hands it to Luis.

Tonight we will dine on capybara tacos with some rice and some beans. This is a feast in the Lost World.

I do not realize it at the time, but as the sun goes down below K-Bar Ridge and the stars become obscured by the approaching rain, we are being watched.

In the morning, we pack up our jungle camp and move up the Iguana River. We camped at a fork in the river the previous night that has now led us to a whitewater river that climbs up to a waterfall near the summit of Sierra Magualida. Dante and I call this river Sierra One.

Making a judgment call, Dante decides to take us farther up the Iguana another ten miles to another mountain river we call Sierra Two.

My guide is certain that Tigre is living with a band of Hoti Indians that have recently settled some gardens in the flat highlands of the massive mountain up Sierra Two, at the summit of Sierra Magualida.

He shows me on the maps back in Puerto Ayacucho about the recent migration of several Hoti bands, separate groups of about twelve to twenty in size, from a river to the west called the Cano

Mosquito. Some disturbance in the tribal group had been causing a rift that sent some of them east into this mountain range.

From what I have learned about the Hoti, the males hunt for their particular band from remote camps. They utilize long blow-guns and darts soaked in a poisonous paste called *curare*, made from the bark of a tree. It was often made by Alberto back in his Piaroa settlement. He used to trade with the Hoti hunters, traveling south into this region by navigating the rivers.

The Hoti would trade bamboo they harvested high in the mountains for blow guns used by tribes throughout Amazonas.

These navigational experiences give Alberto priceless experience to help locate Tigre. I also find out that Beto has experience guiding Special Operations Forces into remote jungle regions throughout Venezuela, Guiana, and Colombia. I understand now why I feel so comfortable around him.

Dante is no dummy; he has been able to utilize his personal knowledge, but moreover, Alberto and others to help access these regions for scientific researchers in recent years.

These researchers are working in regions in the lower Asita River range here, and over to the west in the Cano Majagua region and the Cano Mosquito Region.

Like a Special Forces Green Beret, Dante has established an amazing network in a vastly unexplored region of relatively untouched indigenous tribes of the Sierra Magualida.

I only hope he has been keeping his promises with them.

By the time we make our second night on the Iguana, I am smoked.

We make great progress in one day, only ten miles, but hard-earned miles.

Over the course of the journey, I have received a total of five stingray bites. Luis has three. Dante and Beto have no injuries. I feel like a magnet for the critters.

Running upriver reminds me of the boat drills we did in BUD/S when we carried our rubber boats over our heads as a boat crew. Everyone has to put out or the other teammates suffer.

I have a tendency to overdo it on the effort and often carry more weight than some others, but I don't know of a great Team Guy who has had a different experience than being That Guy.

I overdid it, and I am suffering the consequences. The stingray bites sure didn't help. It is not so much the pain of five hammers crushing my lower legs, but the dime-sized wounds are red and itchy. Their round heads are swelling and pussing up. I run to my med bag on the boat and fish out my precious supplies. I desperately need to open, wash, irrigate, and dry these wounds and let them heal in the night air. When I get to my supplies in the boat I open my blue bag and to my horror find everything in the kit in disarray.

Luis has gone through my kit during our break for lunch.

He must have pilfered my supplies when I took a nap earlier. Everything is gone. The Neosporin tube is empty, I am missing my irrigation tip from my syringe, and all the saline is gone. Not a drop is left. All my aspirin is gone and a bottle of antibiotics has been emptied.

I am crushed.

I charge over to Dante and show him my kit.

"Marco, don't worry, man. These guys do not have the same sense of belonging up here," he tells me. "They adopt the same principles as the Hoti in some respects. There is no sense of ownership. Everything is community. But Luis and some of my other guys don't differentiate from responsibility to the community." Dante grips my shoulder with his right hand. "I learned you have to let some of these things go, Marco. It's just the way it is up here if you don't guard your stuff."

I don't buy it.

"Dante, you can't let them get away with the little stuff like that, man. It adds up to the making a difference on the big stuff later. It will bite us all in the ass. Now I have to pay the price. Do we need him up here? We can drop him off with the Enepa back there and pick him up later."

"No, *chamo*, we will need all hands for the next section up the mountain tomorrow, it gets dangerous up ahead."

"That's what I am afraid of. I learned it in the military, Dante. You let them get away with little things and one day, it's a big blow up and they kick your head in when you least expect it."

"Okay, Marco, but don't make a scene up here. Just watch your stuff, we need Luis for the rapids ahead in Sierra Two."

"Roger that, Dante."

I sleep away from the group that night. Alberto ends up making a quick lean-to out of palm leaves, branches, and vines next to my hammock. It is a gesture of friendship, as he knows I am upset with Dante and Luis.

A gentle rain begins to fall and I stir from my nest and listen to the drops intermittently striking the taut nylon canopy over my bed.

I watch Alberto making the lean-to, his shirt and trousers completely soaked through. He works on the little house with the shotgun still slung over his shoulder. It says a lot for him to be out in the jungle with me and so far from the boat.

Although I know he doesn't like it out here because of the jungle cats, I find out later he knows we are being followed. He is being more than a companion tonight; he is my guardian.

I get out of my dry bed, take off my dry underwear, put on my wet surf trunks, and step into my wet canvas boots. I do not think they have been dry for more than two consecutive days now for several months. I squish my talcum-covered feet into them and adjust my shorts, my body retracting from the cold, wet fabric.

I have thoughts of swimming up on ocean beaches with Doc and Charlie Platoon in our wetsuits on some cold nights as Navy SEALs. I remember Doc throwing heavy 50 horsepower boat motors and running them up into the hinterland and over the soft sand, then us beginning our patrol. The worst part was coming back to the beach, prepping the boats, and putting on our wet neoprene suits.

Brrrrrrr.

The rain washes off my baby powder in cakes as I approach my friend.

"Que pasa, Beto?"

"I sleep inland tonight, Marco. This area dangerous."

"Why is that?"

"It's complicated, *chamo*. You sleep. You need it. You don't look so good today. You're pale like a ghost."

"No shit. I feel fine," I mock. He doesn't get the joke.

"You look sick," he says, giving me a onceover.

"No, man, it's the talcum powder."

"Oh, you scared me, chamo. Anyway, you need rest. Tomorrow much harder."

"Show me how you make that lean-to. That thing is cool."

Alberto teaches me the ropes on making a proper lean-to like the Hotis do. It is a simple square structure of straight bamboo type poles he plucks out of the forest with a loop of his machete. He collects large banana leaves and shows me where to find the vines on the right trees all in a couple of minutes.

"Never saw you make one of these, Beto. How come?"

"Not necessary. Different journey now. Get used to this up here. It starts to get colder at night as we start to climb."

"Cool, Beto. Thanks."

I climb back into my hammock after I go through my powder routine once more. I make a note to keep all of my baby powder well guarded from Luis.

Alberto tucks himself into his lean-to, sits cross-legged inside facing outward, and places his shotgun in his lap.

I can see the whites of his eyes in the darkness.

I feel safe. For the first time I see Alberto for what he is.

He is a Guardian.

Sir Peter Blake, Doc Fullerton, and the many others along the path of my life have been the same. The Guardians show up to test me. If I pass, they take me to the next stage of my journey; they keep me safe.

I shudder at the thought of the challenge in front of me with Alberto. Whatever the challenge may be, I fear it may be my last.

I don't think he bought the talcum powder comment. Maybe I don't look all that great. I won't admit it to myself, but as I relax, I don't feel so good. I am hopeful sleep will help.

I sleep more soundly than I have in weeks.

When I wake, Beto is still sitting in his lean-to, his shotgun still on his lap.

"Good sleep, Marco?" he asks when he sees me.

"Really good sleep."

"*Tranquilo*, Marco." My protector rouses himself up from the jungle floor.

I jump out of my hammock after Beto gets up and wanders off. My legs are in excruciating pain when my feet hit the ground.

Ohhhh shit!

Incredible pain from the wounds…they are getting worse. The swollen red knobs of each entry wound are starting to fester.

I massage my legs above the wounds and check for signs of cellulitis. If that kicks in, I am in big trouble. So far it is just swelling, pain, and itching.

I open my med kit and I pull out what is left of my iodine. One more scrub left in it.

I find a roll of horse tape—an elastic bandage used to tape horses' lower legs. The tape is waterproof and elastic, and it sticks

to itself. I wrap my legs with it to help protect the wounds from abrasions, careful not to wrap too tight and cut off circulation.

After a quiet breakfast, we aim the bow of the crocodile east and up Sierra Two. I can see the top of Sierra Magualida in the distance.

The time is about 5:00 am. The sun is peeking over the mountain top and the clouds are hovering over its cap.

It is a long way up.

SIERRA TWO CAMP

THE FERRYMAN

Sierra Two, Amazon
Sierra Magualida, Venezuela
SUMMER 2001
AUTHOR AGE: 34

Dante leaves Alberto and me back on the beach, laughing at the fact that he does not have to climb up and over the knife ridge along the steep river bank as we do.

The bongo is now much lighter in weight and he can adjust the position of the wooden vessel with much more ease since the extra weight is now out on the river bank.

I see Luis standing up in the boat to lessen the impact of the large chop water on his lower spine and Dante tells the large man to sit down.

The fuel drum in the back of the boat carries the most weight, along with Dante and the motor. The fulcrum of the pitching bow in the waves is equalized, as long as Luis stays up near the bow and keeps it from pitching up to the sky.

Dante knows the river well. Spotting a large standing wave on the steepest navigable section of the river right in front of him, he powers through the swirling water of the eddy and aims the bow at the V-shape of the standing wave. This is the deepest water, and the prop will not strike the smooth rocks under the turbulent river.

The middle-aged Venezuelan explorer is bursting with adrenaline.

One more set of rapids left.

The standing wave ahead of him seems to grow with the increased sound of its roar. At the last moment before the turbulent water of the eddy bounces the bow sideways, Dante guns the boat motor for everything it is worth. The bongo lurches forward and buckles in the bubbling, boiling cauldron below the massive wave. The wave grows at least to eight feet in height above the surface of the river beneath it, but Dante is committed.

Luis jumps to a standing position near the front of the boat. The lurching action from the increased RPMs of the motor and the turbulent water knock him off balance. When the bow hits the standing wave, he is thrown backward and crashes into the fuel can and the bow now launches straight into the sky.

Luis collapses into Dante like a sack of potatoes. The force knocks Dante overboard and into the river before he can let go of the throttle of the motor. In an instant, he is floating down the river in a swirling eddy of the cold water of the mountain. The bongo rights itself and circles back around for him in the current. The motor is still running thanks to the throttle lock he rigged for the outboard.

It helped us a lot in the long transits, and now it keeps the boat circling so he can try to catch it as it comes around to him.

He sees Luis trying to stand up in the boat, not on the motor to shut it down.

The bow approaches Dante quickly and catches him by surprise.

He is wearing his tall snake boots to avoid the stingray bites and they are difficult to swim in. He kicks anyway. His shirt is catching the water and holding down his arms like lead weights just as bad as his boots. He raises his hands up and catches the bow of the wooden dugout as it approaches his place in the boiling bathtub. His hands grip the boat and his boots slam into the mossy hull. He's now cradling the boat with his legs and his belly.

He loses his grip on the slippery wood of the bow and the boat carries over the top of him.

Gasping for air, he gets pushed under the passing hull and quickly raises his head to the surface as soon as he can. His neck and chin are met by the spinning propeller of the outboard motor. Blood fills the water.

Luis pulls him into the boat like a gaffed fish and he crawls into the bow area grasping his throat and gasping for air.

Ignoring his pleas for air, Luis moves to the boat motor and directs the vessel downstream. Expecting him to land the boat on the nearby shoreline, I watch incredulously as he runs the boat full throttle downriver and past my position.

We are four days away from a medical facility or a phone. We need to radio for help.

I found out later Dante lived for two more days, screaming in pain while Luis mindlessly drove on.

I am dizzy and my face is flushed. It feels like I have run into a wall of ice and someone is pinching my nose closed. I begin to vomit uncontrollably.

I feel the flush of cold and heat in my face and throughout my body, and recognize the fever I had been fighting all day. The sickness has kicked in full force. I am at my lowest point physically than I have ever been.

"Marco, *mira!*" Beto says.

"I saw it, Beto. I saw everything." I feel like a shipwreck survivor, lost on a deserted island

Beto and I are now alone and abandoned in the jungle. It feels like someone has kneecapped me at my most vulnerable moment.

"That's impossible. No way that just happened, Beto!" I exclaim to my friend.

Alberto utters an expletive in a language I do not recognize. "We're on our own, *chamo.*"

Luis and Dante are gone...with the radio. Alberto and I are alone in the jungle.

We are stranded. And I am sick.

LOSS OF A FRIEND

Sierra Two—The River of Death
SUMMER 2001
AUTHOR AGE: 34

I am sick to my stomach with fever, but also at the thought of Luis leaving us behind.

As sick as I am, I could have worked on Dante. I still have some of my medical supplies, and I could have helped him. I still had the surgeon's kit Doc gave me with various stainless steel clamps, scissors, and scalpels, all still sterilized. Worst case scenario I could cauterize any wound and pack it and keep direct pressure as we make our way back down to the airfield. Keep him warm and from going into shock, elevate his legs, talk to him, and keep him hydrated.

We could get down to the airstrip, set up camp, and radio for help from the Guardia Nacional, or at the least radio into Wayumi Airlines at Manapiari/Puerto Ayacucho and have them send a Dornier aircraft in.

The Guardia Nacional would have sent a helicopter for him. Everyone knew Dante, and no one would want to face the wrath of his wife if she knew they delayed even seconds.

I do know one thing. Luis does not know how to operate the radio.

The mission below was empty of the Presbyterian missionaries, so no radio there. Luis will have to make it all the way to Manapiare, at least three days downriver.

Shit.

Judging by the look of things, my guide is a dead man.

Alberto is completely bereft. For the first few hours he sits on the edge of the river with his feet in the water and cries into his hands.

I think of Dante's wife, and my heart sinks into my stomach. She told me to watch out for him, to keep him safe, to protect her husband.

I feel completely out of control. I think that I am truly a control freak, in that I always have a clear picture of where I am and what I am doing. I try to visualize my life and my actions before things happen so that I will always have a plan. It seems like the worst things happen to me when I am down. The worst times for things to happen.

If I was on top of my game, I would have been in the boat with Dante. I know it was too far away and happened too fast, but my hatred for Luis burns like a road flare.

I think of Dante's daughters and I cry with Alberto in the river. I should have seen it coming with that guy.

Day begins to turn to night, the growing cumulus clouds filling the sky for an evening rainstorm.

Alberto makes a camp for us. He chops down some straight bamboo branches, lashes them together with vines, gets some wide banana leaf palms and some giant ferns for the roof, then lays some palm leaves down for a mattress.

The clouds have come in during our camp-building and it has begun to rain, a steady patter on the roof. We have the shelter up just in the nick of time.

I stop heaving from nausea and settle into a ravaging fever, now in full force.

Alberto brings in my pack and pulls out some dry clothes for me. I take off my shirt in the dry space of the lean-to and shiver uncontrollably. The air is cooler up here on the mountain.

I change out of my wet clothes, and I get flashbacks to SEAL training and also my earlier years as a Force Recon Marine. The familiar feeling of being wet and muddy stays with me for life, as it does for many veterans.

Naked, I shiver violently. My muscles lock up and I curl into a fetal position, drifting off into a dream I had as a young kid.

I was back in the pond behind my house in Scituate. I swim in the pond and visualize swimming alone in the warm waters of the coastal wetlands.

Back on land, I am tucked into a writhing ball in my makeshift jungle bed. Alberto helps dry me off with my camp towel and puts an emergency blanket from my med kit over me. He places the towel on my forehead and chants in a language I do not understand.

My body heat collects against the aluminum covered plastic of the blanket and my muscles relax enough to help put my mind on better thoughts, in better places.

In my dream, it's the leopard seal at 70 South, the form that represents the Beast.

The shadow is relentless and I cannot shake it. The Beast blows bubbles in my face and presses its massive body against mine under the ice. It grabs my throat and holds me under the surface of my pond. I cannot breathe.

I have a vision of my captain Sir Peter Blake, he is in a bathtub full of water and he is pale white.

I wake up in a fit.

Alberto is sitting under a tree, his shotgun on his lap, staring out into the jungle.

He is on watch and tonight I am safe.

I drift back into a restless sleep, unable to shake the feeling that something is following me on my journey into the Amazon, as if it has never left me from the bow of *Seamaster* on my captain's worst night at sea.

I hope this is as bad as it gets.

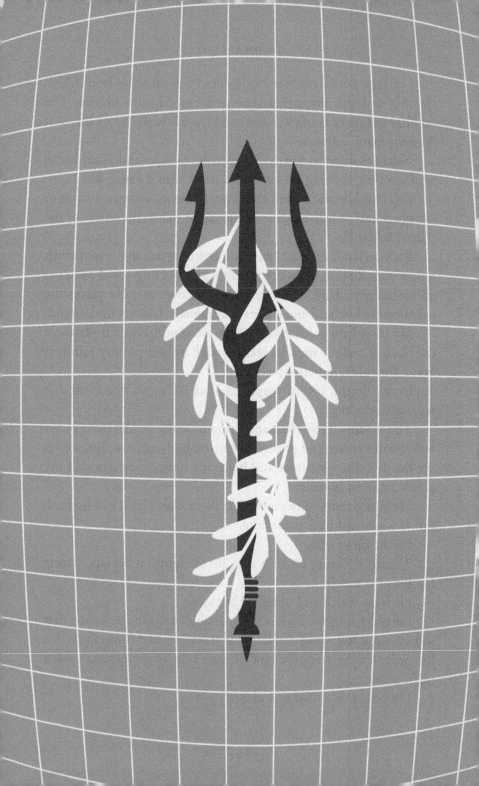

THE LOST CHILD

Sierra Magualida, Amazonas
SUMMER 2001
AUTHOR AGE: 34

At some early hour of the morning, I am awakened. I do not know why I raise my head up out of my warm blanket, but when I do it is still dark, obviously in the early hours of the morning.

It is still raining, a steady rhythm of heavy raindrops cascading in a slow cadence on the lean-to roof. The air is cold and anything wet makes me uncomfortable.

A trickle of water streams through the protective canopy and onto my forehead. I start to move from under my blanket and begin to shiver. I tuck myself in, the slick plastic clinging to my skin.

I vow that I am one day going to make a blanket like this that is comfortable on my skin.

My shaking calms to a shudder and I hear Alberto talking in a garbled tone. His intonations are not like the song I heard earlier but are more guttural and sharp.

I peel the blanket from my eyes and see a tiny angel staring into my eyes. As if in a dream, I study the dark, almond-shaped eyes of an indigenous girl and trace the dark features of her face up to a large tuft of unkempt hair on top of her head.

Curiously, I notice her hair moving and I make out the shape of what at first appears to be a large mouse bobbing up and down in her thick black mane. The hairy creature's eyes pop out from its hiding place and it opens its mouth in a silent shriek, to expose tiny pointed teeth.

I jump up out of my bed. "What the—"

"Marco, stay still," Alberto calls out. "*Tranquilo, tranquilo.* We have a visitor."

As I come to my senses, I make out the little girl hovering over my hammock. She has a tiny monkey in her hair.

The picture is quite adorable. No more than ten-years-old, the girl is wearing a large set of colored beads around her neck and shoulders in a bandolier fashion.

I can't take my eyes off of the marmoset monkey in her hair. I have seen them before, as they are fairly common in the Amazon. It is just amazing to see one living in the girl's hair up here in this lost world. I wish I was in better health and in better spirits to enjoy the moment.

A wave of nausea hits me, but the inquisitive look of her monkey causes me to laugh and the nausea fades. The marmoset has the face of a tiny old man.

Its face is framed by a tuft of white hair that extends an inch into the air, like the plumes of a dandelion. The monkey exudes a musky, earthy scent that brings to mind the smell of a meadow in the mountains of Colorado.

Alberto moves to my side opposite the girl. "Marco, she is separated from her group. They will be looking for her."

"Is she okay?" I ask, evaluating her physical condition.

She is no more than sixty pounds, wears a tattered piece of cloth around her waist, and she has dirty Hobbit feet.

Obviously, a wanderer.

Next to her is a large tan woven basket containing several items wrapped in banana leaves. The contents of the basket smell fruity and pungent.

Honey.

Some of the banana leaves move and I am hit with hunger pains at the thought of food. It is a good sign.

"She is fine. They have been following us upriver for several days. From what I have seen they are a Hoti gathering party."

"Not hunters?"

"No, I think two elders and several children. They gather honey and crabs near the rivers and return to their camps in the highlands. I think she has taken an interest in you and left the group to get a closer look."

"Yeah, she got that all right. Why didn't you warn me?"

"I thought it might cheer you up."

"Very funny, how long has she been here?"

"An hour."

"What do we do now, Beto?"

"We wait for the group to catch up. They won't be far behind."

The girl goes to work rocking my hammock from side to side, and I drift off to sleep again.

When I wake hours later, Alberto is talking with another dark shape at the base of his tree. At first I think it is Dante.

I bolt up. The figure is too small and wiry to be either Dante or Luis.

My heart sinks, but my adrenaline races.

Alberto has his shotgun off to the side and does not even have it in his hands. His machete is up against the tree sitting idle.

The man is clearly a friend.

I shift under my protective canopy and get a better view of the obvious form of a naked man squatting while conversing with my guide.

The indigenous man cuts a figure that is alien to me. He has an unusually large head, with a dense crop of dark hair covering his dome like the large conical hat of the Orient. His dark, wiry build is at ease in his squatting posture.

I cannot help but notice he has an incredibly hairy back that forms a large hump near his shoulders, and gradually my weary brain processes he is wearing a dead pig over his shoulders.

It is a small jungle peccary that he must have killed. He has the two front legs bound by some sort of twine to make the creature into a backpack of sorts.

The man shifts his weight on his haunches and I notice a crossed bandoleer of beads over his chest.

I am grateful they are not bullets.

I am happy to find beads over bullets anytime in the wilderness, especially when involved in affairs concerning the possibility of cannibals and headhunters.

The man shifts his back toward my position in the hut. His naked balls have found a soft leaf on the jungle floor on which to perch themselves. They are safely out of the soil and away from any sharp branches. Obviously a well-chosen landing pad for the man.

I do not call attention to myself and allow the men to talk without distraction. My survival could be at stake.

The man has a large blowgun in his right hand and is obviously a hunter. I do not know where the rest of his companions are, though no doubt are watching my every move.

Alberto has my shotgun and machete propped outside of my hooch in plain view. I will not go near the weapons.

Alberto halts his quiet conversation with the man. It seems they are talking in a low voice for my benefit me, as not to wake me up.

I hear kindness in both of their voices.

Alberto takes leave of the man with a simple gesture and moves to my side, some twenty feet away from his tree.

"Marco, we must leave now."

"What's up?"

"This is El Tigre. We can shelter with his group, but it is important we move now. There may be a large storm coming that will flood the trails above." Alberto points toward the summit of Sierra Magualida some 3,000 feet above us.

"Beto, I'm hurting, man."

I peel aside my blanket and pull out my legs. They are both red and swollen at the calves. I am deathly worried cellulitis is creeping into the wounds and spreading down to my ankle and up to my knees. If untreated, this bacterial infection could lead to major complications out here.

"Does he have a boat?" I ask.

"Not here. He can help us over to the other side of the mountain that you call Sierra One on your map. We can float down from there."

"I can't move my ankles." I press on the swollen skin around my feet.

"El Tigre can help us. He is in front of a small group. They've been looking for the girl."

Alberto motions to the diminutive man and he shifts the weight of the dead pig over his shoulder and onto the wet soil at his feet. The pouring rain drips from his dark hair and cascades over his shoulders and upper torso. He is decorated in blotches of black paint, like the spots of a jungle cat.

The man makes a motion and a troop of adolescent children emerge from the forest led by a small, rotund woman wearing an amazing assortment of beads, and gourds and various cotton sacks and leather pouches around her torso.

The woman has a walking stick that she uses as a staff, her bare breasts swaying as she waddles toward me. The children fall into place behind her on a narrow, almost indiscernible path through the forest. This is a real world Hoti path that I have only seen once before. The Hoti are an elusive people. They are like Hobbits.

El Tigre places his blowgun on the ground and shifts a leather sack in front of his chest, removes a piece of bamboo, and places it to his mouth. He sits on the ground and brings his feet together in toward his torso as if he is a human cradle and begins to play music through the primitive looking flute.

His feet are terribly disfigured, warped and twisted inward at the big toes as if he has spent a lifetime climbing trees. They actually are funny little feet.

While he plays his music, the older woman approaches me with warmth in her eyes and a large smile on her face.

The young children follow closely behind her, in a tight formation.

The woman is wearing a natural fabric loincloth over her privates, just like some of the other children.

The little ones behind her are a mix of boys and girls, all completely bare except for a few random pieces of handmade fabric and crossed bandoleers of bright colored beads of reds, blues, and greens over their chests.

In patrols as a SEAL, I had experiences with Indios in the jungle like this when I was with Doc, but this is by far the most remote and primitive I have ever experienced.

Thank you, God, for the simple pleasures.

The Hoti woman touches me and settles into a squatting position by my side. She does not have far to go to get there, as she has relatively low clearance from the ground. The children gather around me in a circle and crowd my space as if it belongs to equally to each and every one of them. The monkey girl moves to her side in a respectful gesture. I decide to call the woman Mama Bird.

Without any regard to my personal space, she opens my blanket to expose my feet and legs. She holds my head and looks into my eyes first, then smells my breath and then my neck and chest. For a moment I feel as if I am an astronaut visiting a foreign planet and being inspected by its inhabitants.

Mama Bird seems captivated by scent as her primary mechanism of greeting and some form of assessment.

The Hoti woman has the most intense smell that I can only describe as honey and flowers, with a mix of a musky smell that has nothing to do with a naturally occurring body odor. She is covered in an oily mixture intoxicating to my senses.

Initially, I was rigid and shivering uncontrollably. I am now more relaxed as she rubs my chest and palpates my abdomen, assessing my condition.

The children have a similar smell but emit a sweet scent of flowers and honey and wet earth. They keep a distance away and watch silently as the rain falls over their bodies. One of them farts.

She gets the first nickname. I call her Little Stinker. I name the monkey girl Little Monk. There is an even younger girl that carries a large dead rodent like a doll; I call her Pig Pen.

With the flute music playing, I reach over to my backpack and rummage for a pair of my Ice Breaker merino wool underwear and a black merino wool t-shirt and cover myself up.

The troop gathers around Alberto and me, and all at once I am overcome by a sense of acceptance of this tribe of little people of the forest.

I am in a circle of jungle Hobbits and I feel safe. I feel a great sense of redemption from my experience in Manaus with the children in the old riverboat. It is like I passed a challenge, and in return I am rewarded.

It is that simple.

TIGER OF THE MOUNTAIN

Sierra Two—Magualida
AUTUMN 2001
AUTHOR AGE: 34

The rain stops and El Tigre stows his flute.

The team gathers up my belongings under the direction of Alberto. I am in no condition to walk, but we move anyway. I walk slowly with the troop as we make our way to higher ground.

During the night we all end up sleeping in a circle under a large tree. Its wide, flat leaves act as an expedient canopy from the steady rain.

My fever pitches and I feel the shaman at my side stroking my forehead and hair. It is a soothing medicine. Some of the children take turns to bring a fresh-cut water vine to my sweaty forehead and my parched lips. There is a constant flood of hands and attention, not much talk.

By midmorning the sun crests over the top of Sierra Magualida.

From our position, I can barely make out the mountain's summit to the east, far above our heads.

The terrain is gradual and sloping in flowing valleys and ridges toward the top of the lush green mountain.

Magualida is not a flat top tepui like many of the other land islands in the Guiana Shield. I am grateful for the flowing terrain we are following at the river's edge. I cannot think of any time that I ever had to be carried out of an adventure.

I still have a scar on my neck from carrying Doc Fullerton's tree trunk of a body out of a live fire ambush we encountered training in the jungles of Panama.

Doc went down and I hoisted him and all his combat gear over my right shoulder. I slung my M4 carbine over my back and Doc's massive weight pressed my flash suppressor up against my neck. I can still smell my flesh sizzling under the white-hot metal of my barrel and its tip.

El Tigre moves out ahead of the pack, scanning the trees. He is not focused on my needs whatsoever. He has a natural indifference to an injured man, as do all the Hoti hunters up here, Alberto tells me.

Injury and sickness come from being out of balance with good spirits and nature. If you are hurt, it is because you have done something wrong.

Alberto tells me the Hoti woman is considered a shaman of sorts.

As it turns out, she was leading the children of their particular group on what amounts to a nature walk, representing a learning journey for the younger ones of the tribe before they come of age within their society. It was Little Monk who broke up the expedition when she wandered off.

Alberto tells me that they are walking to known beehives to harvest honey within the valley of this river that I call Sierra Two. El Tigre serves as the guide and point man for the scrappy jungle patrol, and also hunts for targets of opportunity for meat.

The shaman and the children function as gatherers on the trek, learning things along the way. Many of the children are carrying woven baskets on their backs, no doubt full of honey.

Now that I am part of the procession, I am off to a difficult start. My ankles are so swollen I cannot get my boots on. I end up wearing my wool underwear as shorts and my wool t-shirt for warmth in the cool mountain air.

The rain captured on the leaves above trickles down and heats my face, the fresh water running into my thirsty mouth.

Finally, we reach a point below a large ridge line. I rub my ankles and flex them as best I can. I get a decent range of motion out of them and begin to walk up the ridge right up behind El Tigre. I feel it is important I am up with him, in front of the pack.

I try as best I can to match him step for step up the tiny trail to the crest of the knife-edge ridgeline.

One evolution at a time.

El Tigre is the perfect man to follow up the trail. He places every foot in the best part of the trail, like he knows each location. He is smooth but fast, so it is closer to following a dance step than a hike.

Walking the trail with him I get a powerful feeling that I am now a Hoti in this Lost World.

Suddenly the obscure trail lives beneath my feet, as if I am scaling the back of a large dragon on a trek up the Lonely Mountain. I know where every scale is placed and where not to step.

I follow Little Monk carrying a large basket that appears full of food. She has a fluffy white feather in each ear as decoration. She and the shaman are obviously picking them up as they find them on the trek. I follow her pace, as she is weighed down and slowest of the group.

El Tigre put her up front with the recognition of the weight she bears in the pack string.

The Hoti girl has been by my side and helping the medicine woman tend my wounds since she found me. She looks back at me many times during the walk and purposely slows for me. Pig Pen is often right behind my heals with her dead rat, it really freaks me out. The pace is slow and it is helpful, since each step feels like I am walking barefoot across broken glass.

Back in SEAL training, running in the sand dunes alongside Andy, Sam, my swim buddy, Gus, and my good friend, Bobby N, all of us were in sync, our feet landing in one another's footprints in the soft sand of Coronado, California. It was like a dance, mile after mile. Head down, keep the flow, never give up.

On a break, Mama Bird takes all the children under her arms and points out various plants and insects. The shaman hosts discussions played out almost entirely in sounds and body language. She occasionally holds out a plant or a bug to smell. She occasionally will crush something and put it into a mixture in one of the containers decorating her body. She seems to have an incredibly adapted sense of smell.

At one point in the journey up the mountain, Mama Bird brings up one of the boys toting a large woven basket, obviously carrying supplies. From within, she pulls out some plantains while Sam and Frodo build a fire. She skillfully mashes the bananas and mixes a few smaller types I recognize as sweet bananas. She draws out a metal cup and cooks the mixture over the fire.

When it is ready, the entire troop sits around in a circle and eats the meal.

I am offered some and I wolf it down with pleasure. I am famished and the meal is equivalent to eating one hundred energy bars while I am in my diminished state.

Little Monk makes it a mission to help feed me along with her marmoset monkey. I feel I have been adopted by her and her friend Pig Pen. I never accept anything offered to eat by the dirtiest of the two.

Alberto stays close to me and offers a water bottle from my pack, I share a sip with the children when gathering around me on breaks. This is a fascinating culture. The kids are not stampeded up the trail, or hen-pecked, or bossed around. They seem to have a natural rhythm of helping one another out. Almost like a flying flock of birds, they constantly adjust themselves to the direction of the flock.

Little Monk was never chastised for wandering off, she simply blended back into the group. It is communal—all is shared.

At this particular stop I am able to sit on my haunches to keep the pressure on my ankles and my blood pumping to my feet. I rock back and forth while I eat, the burnt banana and honey soothing my throat. A moderate rainstorm has come and gone during the walk up the ridgeline, and the bugs are starting to come out again.

I feel a quick slap on one of my swollen ankles and almost jump up in pain and surprise. Little Monk is swatting away tiny bloodsucking gnats that are attacking the swollen flesh around my wounds.

I quickly assess she has made a mission out of keeping bugs away from my bites and I smile, even though I wince at every slap. I find it endearing.

El Tigre takes the time to join the fire and tell a story to the group while we eat. It is a story of hunting and conquest in the jungle, obviously chasing his prey and killing it.

The children are amused by the story, and Mama Bird chops another water vine and pours it on my forehead.

Alberto spends a quiet moment with me before we step out again.

"Marco, we will be at their settlement by nightfall if you keep your pace. You are doing well."

"Yeah, Beto, the Hoti woman is amazing."

"Marco, she is a *Kajo jau!*"

"Huh?"

"She is a visionary, a shaman."

"I had a feeling. She definitely has the bearing of someone special in the group. Beto, thanks for the watchful eye."

"*Si, chamo.* We will finish this in memory of Dante. He would want this."

"You think he's dead?"

"I do. I saw his spirit pass on the river. I think you saw it in your dreams, you were twisting and moaning in your sleep."

"What's next?"

"We make it to their village and ask Tigre to join our quest to Aracamoni."

The air is getting cooler the higher we climb. My feet are in excruciating pain. Blisters have begun to form and the skin is peeling off of my heels. What used to be strong calluses are now mush.

I get my long-sleeved shirt out of my backpack that one of the kids is carrying for me. I retrieved my shotgun from Alberto and carry it myself.

When we finally traverse the sharp ridgeline, we drop into an open valley at the convergence of two rivers deep within the shadow of Magualida, now towering above.

The Lone Mountain.

In the center of the valley is an opening in the canopy where a large communal house built entirely of palm thatch from the jungle is sitting. It is not as big as some other Indio lodges I have seen in my adventures across South America, the largest being the Yanomami. They have huge roundhouses with courtyards in the center of flat dirt, where they have celebrations, dances, and communal meetings.

This is just one large hut, about twenty feet tall and forty feet long by thirty feet wide. It brings to mind a jungle version of a Hobbit house. The hut is covered with huge leaves that look like giant ferns, and has a narrow doorway through the massive leaves that lead inside. The flame of a fire dances at a hearth within the narrow slice of blackness. The remaining community of male and female adults exit the structure upon our approach.

All in all there are about twenty tribespeople living within this giant hut.

All of them are wearing the characteristic beaded necklaces, curious and yet wondrous decorations of the tribe.

The beads that make the necklaces are made from seeds of various plants, which give them deep, rich colors.

None of the others have the ornate decorations of Mama Bird. The old woman not only has her decorative amulets around her neck, but she also found some long, dark feathers and inserted them in large piercings in her earlobes. She is covered in dirt from the trek, but still ornate as compared to the simple decorations of beads with the others.

I sit by a tree and rest while Alberto talks with the main group.

I see some concern with the men and women of the village about my condition. One points down to Mama Bird's hut, about one hundred meters to the south. Alberto collects me and the girl and we follow the shaman down to our nest for the night.

Mama Bird now has a child, no more than two years old, tucked under her arm and held to her chest. She walks cradling the child and leads us down the hill to her place near a babbling brook.

When we arrive at her house, I am not invited in, but shown a place to tie my hammock outside the main door.

Alberto lets me get settled in and helps with my hammock from my ruck and a waterproof tarp over my head. I drape a mosinet over my bed, and I am set.

My fever is still raging and my legs are in horrible shape. The food from the camp earlier in the day gave me enough energy to make it to my bed tonight.

I fall asleep, and sometime later Alberto calls me to the upper camp where they have a meal being prepared. It is dark and the jungle is alive with a cacophonous sound of insects.

Apparently, there is a celebration tonight.

When we arrive, the peccary is over the top of an open fire just being cooked whole, the smoke rising from various points in its carcass.

Other food is presented to me, which included ground maize and a soup made from palm nuts called lute. These nuts are roughly the size of olives and are eaten in copious amounts. I understand the need for protein and the delicious taste of roast meat and fat on the bone. Up here, I know I cannot touch the protein they cook in any way.

Earlier, I noticed one child who I nicknamed Frodo having difficulty with his bowel movements.

TMI alert: It is a lot of fun to poop in this wilderness.

It is often done as a group in an area downstream of gathering water and bathing, thank God.

We would squat in knee-deep water, and as each of us did our business, little fish would appear from nowhere to eat everything that launched into the water from the torpedo tube. It is the weirdest feeling when they come up and nibble right on your water tight O-ring. It is very efficient.

Fortunately, there are no piranha up here in the fast-moving water. In the lower elevations, I often see girls and women with scars on their legs and thighs from the carnivorous fish going for them during "that time of the month."

Doc Fullerton would often work with Indios we encountered in our SEAL adventures by helping medicate communities with field clinics he would set up to administer basic drugs or pull bad teeth.

Pork in the Amazon is notorious for carrying worm larvae, so cooking must be particularly careful and complete. If it's not cooked enough, the larvae that attach themselves to the muscles of the animal grow into worms in your belly.

I once saw Doc pull a tapeworm out of the tail end of a child, and I never want to remember it again. It was like something out of an alien movie. He made me grab the slippery body of the worm and pull. It felt like the grossest, hardest, most snakelike, yuckiest thing I ever touched.

Blugggh.

The other concern I have for meat is the curare the Indios use to kill prey. If it exists in the protein it can kill me or make me violently ill. I pass on the peccary.

After the group sits and begins to eat, a flute is played by one of the adults and the song bounces off of the surrounding trees and canopy above like a natural Bose system.

Alberto points out one of the adults that I nickname Big Foot, for obvious reasons. He is slightly fatter than the other adult males and he moves into the center of the group around the fire.

Alberto tells me Big Foot happens to be the worst hunter in the group, but he is known to be the best storyteller when it is time to eat by the fire. He makes up for his lack of hunting prowess with the strength of prose.

Dancing to the sound of the flute behind him, Big Foot launches into an animated story for the tribe. Apparently it is a story of a jungle cat, the dreaded jaguar, that pursues him, and Big Foot eludes it by throwing a large stick at it. He bends down and picks up a large fire log and throws it out to the dark jungle beyond the illumination of the jungle where it burns in the darkness.

El Tigre makes a rhetorical joke by picking up his spear and mimicking himself throwing it with the pointy end at the beast and killing it. The crowd bursts into happy laughter.

The Hoti tribe does not call him El Tigre. That is a lowland term in the Spanish language spoken by the Venezuelans and the missionaries. Up here they call him Jau.

Beto tells me that to the Hoti, jau are considered witches. They wander the jungle and only hunt, they do not tend gardens. Beto points to Little Monk in the corner, asleep in her hammock with the toddler.

"She calls the girl *Uli kwayo*. A monkey person."

"No shit?"

"Yes. She is not considered *Ni jodi*—a real person—in their belief system. It is why she is held separate from the others, and why she is with the shaman...like the little one with the rodent."

"That explains a lot."

Alberto has proven to be priceless on this scouting expedition ever since Dante died. Tonight, he saves the expedition. It turns out that he and El Tigre have worked with Dante and Lucho in the past.

The two discuss previous expeditions in the region by scientists from around the world, and also smuggling fuel into Colombia. I should have paid more attention to their conversation, it would have helped me in the future.

During the campfire that night, Tigre, Alberto, and I come up with a plan. When I am able to hike again, Alberto will travel down the mountain with me and fall back on Lucho to help build the logistics with me for the trip.

In October, Beto will meet El Tigre down in Manapiare at the appropriate time and take him down the Rio Ventuari near La Esmeralda as the Blakexpeditions jungle team is making our way up the Casiquiare River.

El Tigre will wait for us in a Yanomami village called Coromoto located at the junction of the Casiquiare Canal and the Siapa River. He will guide us to the goldmine on Aracamoni when we arrive.

With the logistics complete and the friendships made around the campfire, I return to my hammock alone that night. I settle in after coating myself in a layer of talcum powder from my ruck.

It feels like heaven.

I pass out for what feels like minutes and wake up several days later, feeling much better, but still in a world of hurt with my feet and lower legs. Although the pain is gone I have a lot of swelling.

The days pass and I watch everyone travel from the hut to the nearby river. Little Monk helps me with food and the shaman fusses over me.

Finally, as a group, we journey down to the whitewater river near the hut and bathe ourselves.

I find a quiet spot on the edge of the water and prop my shotgun up to a tree.

I strip down and enter the water in a cove, letting the cool mountain water soothe the swelling in my legs. My pain goes away completely under the water.

It is a feeling of absolute joy.

I am in my own Garden of Eden, and for the first time in many days I feel strong enough to hike again.

Beto puts a black bag on the edge of the water and nods to me. I swim over to my med kit, open it at the edge of the water, and lay out its contents on a large rock.

It isn't much in the way of supplies.

I find some anti-bacterial scrub and horse wrap tape, scrub my wounds, and put bandages over the soft scrubbed scabs after I clean out all the pus. After, the pressure is released from both my calves and I have better mobility in my ankles.

I dry off in the sun for a bit and let the sun warm my body before the troops move out.

More days pass and eventually I am ready to travel. When Beto makes the announcement there is little fanfare.

The shaman and Little Monk pack their belongings into large woven baskets and we all move up the mountain in proper formation.

So far we have traveled about five miles from the accident on the river to Camp One as I call it. Today we will hike three miles up the mountain to Camp Two that Beto describes as a garden site they use to gather sweet potatoes and maize.

We will link up with the river—Sierra One—then hike downhill and pick up a bongo near the confluence of the Iguana and the mission.

I am wearing my waterproof rucksack, my olive drab cargo pants, my jungle shirt, and my white floppy hat, as well as a pair of Teva sandals I threw in the bottom of my pack back in Puerto Ayacucho when I emptied everything out.

We hike all day from the camp and make it into the highlands of the Lost World.

Mama Bird waves a hand out to a large stand of bamboo within which the camp is built. This apparently used to be where a village elder lived. He would trade various bamboo stocks used for blowguns by the communities below.

According to Alberto, the shaman is a village chief of sorts.

At the camp, Beto gets directions to Sierra One from one of the tribesmen. I am eager to get moving back to the lower elevations. We are currently 3,000 feet above sea level and it is noticeably cooler up here.

Without celebration, we leave the summit and head down the mountain. El Tigre, Mama Bird, and Pig Pen join us down the mountain. Little Monk stays behind to catch crabs with a pack of young girls.

At the boat, Beto and I paddle into the mist rising from the cold water of river and head back to Manapiare. It is a bittersweet ending for such an arduous trek...but for this tribe there is no hello and goodbye, it is merely sharing the path.

When I return to Puerto Ayacucho I head directly for Dante's house, where we confirm he has died. It is an extremely emotional moment. We put our heads together in prayer for a husband, father, and friend.

Lena introduces me to Ana Carolina, a close friend of the family, who offers me a guest house while she works on family affairs with the girls. This is the perfect place to get strong again.

The bungalow sits on stilts above the jungle and has a covered deck that overlooks the giant Rio Orinoco, and also has an awesome waterfall nearby from a tributary from the surrounding hills.

I am in paradise. I spend my time recovering in a hammock while Ana plays the guitar. We pass the few days we have together in peace and harmony.

When Lena and the girls join us, we all end up coming back to the waterfall and laying back into the flowing water of the river. It is an amazing waterfall, a gradual pitch of smooth granite rock, and the waterfall is actually only several inches of water cascading over its wide surface.

We lay down on our backs and the water jets over our bodies in a sheet of warmth.

In the distance a lightning storm forms and we watch the dancing bolts in the sky from a safe distance. It is an amazing show, and an amazing experience.

I play with Dante's children in an obstacle course I found earlier in the waterfall. The entire length of the course is about one hundred yards in length, with a moderate pitch. I scout the course myself to determine its safety and lead the entire group on the adventure when I have it plotted.

Dante's wife tells the children to follow me through the flowing watercourse. The children and I slide through a cascade of water chutes and ladders, encountering obstacles of slippery, moss covered wormholes bored through the prehistoric rock of the Orinoco. The holes are big enough to drive a car through, and small enough at points where we lay on our backs and slide with the warm waters of Amazonas, like a natural water slide. It is not steep enough to be dangerous, and the water is only twelve inches deep over the rocks. The slide's course terminates in a clear water pool in a large cave.

The final challenge is to hold our breath and swim down to an illuminated passage, a hole in the rock about six feet below the surface, about six feet in diameter. It leads to another clear water pool and cave surrounded by ferns and other jungle plants. It is like a scene from *Jurassic Park*, and is absolutely beautiful.

All of us float in the deep water of the first pool and I take the ladies by their hands and cross the obstacle, one at a time. Dante's two daughters want to swim the obstacle together.

I take the hands of the two girls and we take a deep breath, swimming together, and pass the threshold to the other side. I hand the two daughters to their mother with tears in my eyes. I remember the words of Matheus back in Manaus on a scary evening as he put his hand in mine. "Encante."

The entire experience brings life back into my body with a strength and determination to finish this quest.

I make plans to link up with Lucho and build our expedition vessel for the crew that I call the Jungle Team. It is a proper catamaran that looks like something out of *Gilligan's Island*. It will support the Blakexpeditions team as well as a Nat Geo film crew for over a month in the rapids. Once complete, Lucho and I will stage fuel drums along our route and hide them in caches and safe houses along the one thousand-mile journey. It is no small task, but compared to my past troubles on my scouting expedition, it is easy.

We name the jungle catamaran *Seamaster II*, and when it is complete and the fuel is staged, it is finally time for me to meet *Seamaster* and my team.

We are ready.

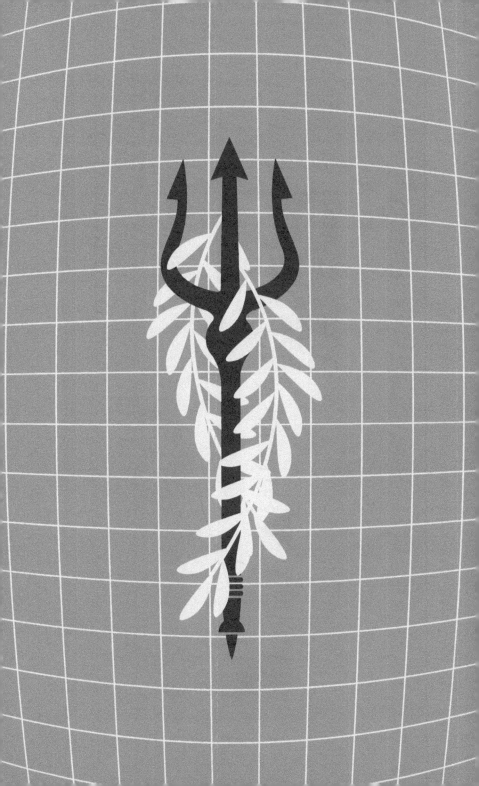

THE JUNGLE TEAM

Blakexpeditions
NOVEMBER 2001
AUTHOR AGE: 35

By the time I meet *Seamaster* and my captain and team, I no longer look at the rivers of the Amazon as a playground. It is changing for the worse.

We had the good fortune of a pleasant transit up the Amazon River and the Rio Negro. The time came for us to depart on the most challenging part of the journey—the trek to find the gold mine of Aracamoni, and take it down.

I am thrown a giant curveball when Sir Peter informs us that he will not be traveling with the Jungle Team, but staying with *Seamaster*. The news is devastating to me.

Once the Jungle Team departs, the captain and his sailing team will be on their own.

I know this weighs heavily on Sir Peter as well. He doesn't think the sailing crew is serious about the risks of the pirates out there and he recognizes the tension between them and me as I was stressing the importance of sentry watch on the bow and stern of the vessel.

I understand why Pete is not going up the mountain with us.

Sir Peter has already confided in me that he does not think the Ozzy captain has the skills to get *Seamaster* back down the river safely.

I talk with my captain extensively about his concerns for the vessel and our secret mission to the mine.

"Climb the mountain with the film crew, radio the captain, top of the world. Over the biosphere reserve, and continue with Tigre to the mine. Film it and get out safely."

"Roger that," is all I have to say.

I know Sir Peter is ecstatic about this leg of the journey, for the expedition as well as personally. He is truly on a mission to make a difference in this world by sharing important signs and symptoms from the pulse points of the planet's health. He lives it daily and through sleepless nights.

When we have a ship's meeting later in the day, I sit down with Ollie and pore over the details of the Jungle Team transit from San Gabriel.

From the last city in Brazil for the Seamaster we will transit via a troop transport along a winding dirt road to Cucuí. It is about one hundred miles, and fortunately, the weather has been dry.

At the meeting for the entire crew, I review the security concerns Doc laid out to me.

The main priority is to have someone on bow watch with a spotlight and a radio back to the pilot house watch from dusk 'til dawn.

The crew will rotate security watches throughout their journey south until they enter the Atlantic Ocean.

It is the same if *Seamaster* is floating in the ice fields of Antarctica or resting in the painted rivers of the Amazon.

Instead of scanning the waters for icebergs, we are now scanning for pirates.

My primary goal for our crew is never to be taken by surprise.

If we have a patrol at night scanning the waters, we portray ourselves as a target that shows vigilance.

If someone decides to try to attack *Seamaster*, we are not going to stop them or ward them off, but we can spot them and alert the remainder of the crew.

My lesson to all is to get everyone onto the decks and toward the bow of the vessel, avoiding the open area of the fantail at all costs. This is where pirates control the crew of the vessel and where bad things happen.

When *Seamaster* pulls into San Gabriel after 1,500 miles into the Amazon Basin, the captain and crew have a big celebration in town that evening.

Miguel has Katia waiting on the wharf when we pull our red Zodiac up to the bustling town. San Gabriel is mostly a military outpost for the Brazilian army, but it has a bustling town center and bars.

Upon hitting land, I give Katia a big hug. Miguel is proud of navigating the vessel up the tricky waterway with his pilot Jack. Sir Peter's wife, Pippa, and their daughter, Sara Jane, are there as well, having flown in on a float plane earlier. Sir Peter is glowing in the presence of his family.

We start with a local dance party Katia has organized for us and have a priceless time getting up and taking turns dancing the rumba and anything else we can invent.

I do not know it at the time, but this will be the last time I spend with my great captain of the sea.

We will laugh, and dance, and drink under a warm Amazonian sky on a starry night.

The evening will end with Janot, Alistair, and me hunting down Ollie in the early hours of the next morning and finding him passed out in an alley with his pants down to his ankles and a Hawaiian shirt stuffed full of fake dollar bills that read "MERMAID DOLLARS" in Portuguese. God only knows what our first mate was up to late in the evening.

It is a classic end of Blakexpeditions as we know it.

This will be the last night we are all together as a crew, as a team.

In the morning, the Jungle Team watches Sir Peter maneuver his ship through the challenging rapids of the Rio Negro. We all know it is a difficult decision that he makes today. Sir Peter Blake's objective lies off a port town at the mouth of the Amazon. Earlier, he plotted *Seamaster's* final anchorage in the Amazon River at latitude 0° 00' 5.428" N and aimed her bow downriver for the port of Macapa.

I smile at the thoughts of us skinning it out of Antarctica in the massive storm we encountered heading north. It was indeed our most challenging night at sea.

Our captain steers *Seamaster* back to the open waters of the Atlantic Ocean. I can tell he is looking forward to stretching his wings over following seas once again.

After a dusty, bumpy transit by military transport to the border town of Cucuí, we have the opportunity to sit down for our first meeting as an independent team.

El Jefe, the Venezuelan film producer, and the Nat Geo filming team join us. At this point the film crew is a two-man team consisting of James, the cameraman, and Simon Atkins, the director.

These two guys have proven themselves extremely versatile in the previous one thousand plus miles of the journey. The next leg will challenge them to the extreme.

"We need to film the Yanomami!" Simon exclaims to the group.

"What's changed since last briefed the storyline?" I ask.

"We just talked with Jefe. He says he has film permits for the Yanomami. We need to utilize that!"

"We are caught in a crossroads out here. The Yanomami by the rivers are too civilized. It'll be boring and nothing different from what tourists are doing back here. It's tailgate camping."

"Why not go deep to the tribe of the Yanomami boys?" Simon points to them, Number One and Number Two, now approaching with the remainder of the Aracamoni team, minus El Tigre.

I take a breather and walk over and give the two boys a big hug, and give a bear hug to Alberto.

Lucho walks up and gives me a hug as well. "All ready, Marco."

"Tigre is up in Siapa?" I ask.

"Yes, but we have to move fast. He is impatient...there are things going on."

"I know, Lucho. Thanks. Great work!"

"Okay, Marco we go fast, careful of Jefe."

"I can see that already, *chamo*."

This calms me down, but my dander is up substantially with Jefe pulling the Nat Geo crew aside and trying to write his own script.

Fortunately, Doc had given me a heads up of a recent massacre in the backcountry. Jefe represents the needs and intentions from Hugo Chavez himself, who is El Presidente at this time.

This is how fast I can lose the expedition; at the drop of a dime if I am not vigilant on my objectives.

"Jefe, working with the civilized tribes does us no good and you know it. We're not up here for your plan. This is our approved plan and we need to execute what we planned for."

"We need to showcase the Yanomami on the rivers and show this as a fun place to visit."

"You can do that on your time and with another crew, Jefe. We're here to film the Biosphere Reserve from Aracamoni."

"What if we go deep into Neblina and film the Yanomami up there that helped build the expedition boat you have down there on the beach? It's a great story."

"Not an option. Too dangerous back there right now."

Jefe knows his plan is quickly falling apart. We are not push-overs, and I know about the massacre of a Yanomami village back there by illegal miners, the rest of the team does not. I do not want to freak everyone out so early in the trip.

"Not an option," says Jefe. "Only permits for Orinoco and Casiquiare groups at this time. Nada mas."

"We go for Aracamoni."

"It's not as beautiful as Neblina," says Simon, rightly so.

"I know Simon, but the story is deeper up on Aracamoni. You will see."

"We need to load up and get moving if we want to make the first camp by dark," Lucho pipes up. "Big storm coming."

"Let's go, all the logistics are in place." Carlos approaches the cantina. "This is Carlos. He checked on all our fuel and supplies up along our route."

Carlos dips his head in greeting. There is something about him that makes all of us slightly uneasy, but he quickly blends himself in with the group, as if invisible.

The skill of a chameleon.

Doc had warned me earlier about him not being vetted.

"Lucho, Carlos has us dialed in right?"

"Yes, Marco, I checked."

"Let's go, gents. The tiger of the mountain awaits!" The meaning of my exclamation goes over many heads.

I claw my hand over my heart as my tiger signal to the two Yanomami boys. They smile and help grab gear.

Once aboard, the Jungle Team aptly names the expedition vessel *Seamaster II*.

After getting the film crew in place with their gear and all our hammocks set under the thatch roof, we stow our bags and Lucho gives everyone a tour of our spaceship. Aft of our living area on the starboard bongo is the kitchen, now in full swing.

Sitting in a pocket is our ship's cook, Tomas. He has a wide stovetop full of pots and frying pans. Above his head hang various green flowery vegetables and baskets of fresh fruits.

"Tienes hambre?" he asks

"Yeah, we're hungry, mate!" Ollie answers in his characteristic swagger.

"Hell yeah!" pipes Janot.

"Good, then I will make you all a soup," Tomas says in broken English.

He grabs a big tin pot, holds it out to his side, and dips it in the river only inches away from his sitting position down in the hulk of the dugout.

He scoops up a large bucket of river water and places it over a propane burner on the stove.

Ollie, Janot, Abbo, and I look at one another with the same silent gasp. It is a collective thought of, *there is no way he just did that.*

Yes, he did.

Life on *Seamaster II* is pleasurable for the team. We motor one hundred miles downstream to our first objective, the Yanomami village of Coromoto. I know this to be the staging area of Tigre, and I do not want to delay in reaching him.

We spend several days altering positions around our jungle expedition platform.

The vessel is performing ideally. She is strong, which is reassuring in the tricky rapids we have to navigate along our circuitous course.

The Yanomami boys man the outboard motors, one on each transom, that Lucho mounted in Estuvio. The boys do a great job keeping her going. Lucho occasionally positions himself on the bow and guides the twins. He gesticulates on the prow like a symphony conductor. He is quite entertaining to watch.

The rain is coming down in sheets, and we all retreat under our canopies. Ollie, Doc Shaw, Janot, Abbo, and I are swinging in our hammocks while the makeshift barge motors down the river.

The Yanomami twins, Number One and Number Two, never show signs of discomfort out in the rain.

Janot, Ollie, and Abbo take turns fishing and collecting supplies at villages we hit along the Casiquiare.

For the most part, we are all alone out here in this wilderness.

Relieving ourselves aboard the boat turns into a funny exercise for us all while we are underway. The head is simply a grass hut built *Gilligan's Island*-style over a hole in the wooden planks that span the stern end of the catamaran. It is super funny to watch members of the team take their turns squatting in the hut.

Ollie has taken it upon himself to toss an old *Playboy* magazine on the floor in the hut.

It is funny seeing it in there until the Yanomami boys start abandoning their motors in autopilot (throttle fixed to full power and tiller tied with string) and disappearing in the grass hut for extended periods of time.

Our journey is a steady drone of boat motors along the painted river, with ever present rapids that are so large we do not have to portage.

The large standing waves and rock formations we encounter are intimidating, but the luxury of staying aboard the catamaran helps the time pass easily.

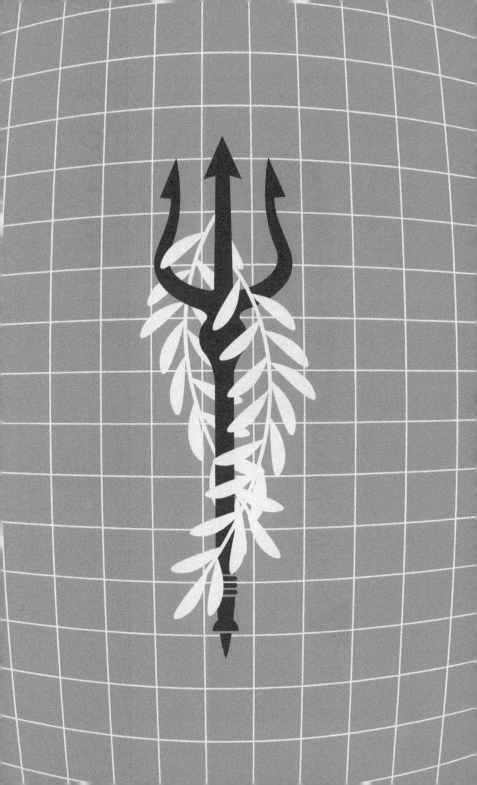

COROMOTO

Rio Casiquiare and Rio Siapa
DECEMBER 2001
AUTHOR AGE: 35

"Sir Peter, we just made the pickup location!" I say into the sat phone.

"Beauty, mate, good luck with your guide."

"Roger, Capitan. I am about to go get El Tigre, we have the film crews running right now."

After a week on the river, we have arrived at our primary staging area to take on the mountain. The riverine environment of the Casiquiare is beautiful, if slightly tedious. The flat terrain around the river does not offer the dramatic relief of the distant lands surrounding the tepuis.

The view is about to change dramatically.

Simon and James film me leaving the expedition vessel. I am wearing a pair of surf shorts and my black Merino wool t-shirt.

As I enter the village, I approach the large village shabono and I am greeted by the village chief and Alberto.

The encounter is slightly awkward since the chief is wearing a suit jacket and tie, but no pants. I rush in and give Beto a big hug.

"Is he here?" I ask him.

"All good, Marco," he responds with a smile.

A swarm of gnats are swarming around the chief's exposed and extremely weathered ankles and I make a personal note to start putting on the bug spray when I feel the gnats on my ankles as well. Not good.

I also notice James and Simon shut down the cameras for this particular encounter.

I move into the hut and find Tigre sitting next to groups of the local tribe, all in various stages of undress.

I nod to Tigre.

A girl bolts out from behind a wooden pole of the structure and runs across the chalky dirt floor of the room. She approaches me where I am squatting on the floor on my haunches. She immediately starts whacking at the bugs assaulting my exposed ankles.

It's Little Monk!

Her appearance and the familiar slapping motion of her hands on my feet bring tears to my eyes. She points up to a new friend while a spider monkey dances in the rafters of the hut.

After everything, we are all together again.

I know all this is Alberto's doing. He joins us for the meeting, and his presence is appreciated. He translates the appropriate thanks to the chief and his people. This community is civilized, in the context of things. Outside, Doctor Marc Shaw is working a makeshift medical clinic with the locals and performing a cursory inspection on the back injury of one of the Yanomami, who is lying in a prone position. The event reinforces the importance of having Doc with us on the journey. Doc Shaw is a great guy and has been a wonderful traveler with us for our journey so far.

Watching him work through the palpation of a medical assessment, I am reminded about Dante and the care we could have given him. If Doc had been up there with me in Manapiare we could have sustained Dante easily.

I think ahead to the next eighty-plus miles we have to cover ascending Aracamoni, and I know that the good doctor is a saving grace for us in case something bad happens up the hill. It's important I keep Doc safe since he is our only hope for a midrange stabilization of any major injuries.

Earlier, in conversations with Sir Peter, my captain cautioned me to make the proper decision when we reached this village and picked up Tigre.

Doc Shaw is relatively unknown to me. He had flown into Brazil specifically to participate with the Jungle Team, and was chosen through conversations with Doc Trevor and Sir Peter. Doc Shaw had no connection to Doc Fullerton or myself.

My judgment call at the moment is to keep Marc Shaw down at Coromoto with Lucho and the boat crew. It is not fair to put our expedition doctor at risk while entering the mine unannounced as we plan to do. Plus, if anything does happen to any of us, the best chance we have would be to get down to him and stabilize while we wait for transport out of Coromoto.

When I announce my intentions to Doc Shaw, he is extremely dejected. He confronts me about the situation while the Nat Geo crew is rolling the film and they capture the entire conversation on the televised program that comes out later.

Ollie volunteers to stay back with Doc after the argument settles without me budging on the issue.

I hurt the doctor's feelings at the moment, but there is no way I can explain my fear of something happening to him up the mountain. I had no training with him and he is our only true medical officer.

The journey up the mountain will be difficult and dangerous. The crew that I am taking up has indeed been through the mixing pot with me. I have Janot and Alistair, and I have been through life and death with my teammates from Blakexpeditions.

Alberto is driving our bongo that we have been towing along with us on the mother ship.

I have Tigre.

That is our full boat.

Lucho and the Yanomami boys will stay behind as the vanguard force for the expedition vessel, leading us out of trouble if we find any, which we are consequently looking to find.

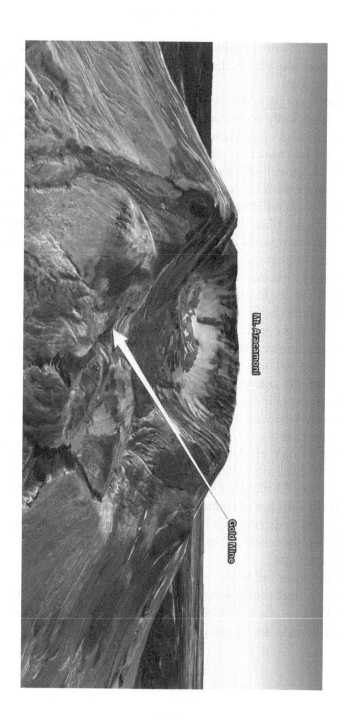

Mt Aracamoni

Gold Mine

THE GOLD MINE

The Lost World with Blakexpeditions
DECEMBER 2001
AUTHOR AGE: 35

The journey up the mountain is perilous. We are way off the beaten path now as we ascend the Siapa River. Alberto has navigated the flat course of the river in the lower sixty miles of twists and turns.

As we begin to ascend into the tepui region, the bugs become unbearable!

"Fuck, mate!" yells Abbo. "I can't see my bloody arm!"

Abbo holds out his right arm, his sleeve rolled up to his elbow exposing his skin—his arm is completely covered in mosquitoes!

Knowing it was going to be tough going with the bugs, I had brought along mosi-net hats that fit over our ball caps to keep the bugs from attacking our faces and necks. The nets are a godsend!

The bugs are brutal, and the portages up the whitewater river become endless. Mile after mile we motor along, stop, lift the boat past the gurgling water and over the slippery rocks, then motor along again.

"No wonder Doc Shaw stayed in Coromoto, mate. Theez eez bloody dangerous."

"At least it's easy to float back downstream if someone gets hurt up here. It's a blessing to have him below if we need him. I learned my lesson the hard way with my guide Dante."

"Yeah, God help us if we do."

"This is crazy!" yells Abbo.

"I know, Abbo. We're only halfway. Don't get discouraged."

"Yeah, the bright side is, it only gets fucking worse," curses Janot.

I nod. "Honestly, it does."

Alberto and Tigre work tirelessly to move the boat up the countless rapids. Our guide keeps his head down and his mouth shut the entire journey.

I know Alberto told him to keep it on the down-low, but Tigre takes it to the extreme. He is processing a lot more internally than externally, I know that for a fact.

I don't distract him from his thoughts. I just hope we can keep up with him when we start to hike up the mountain.

"Holy sheet! This guy is hauling ass, mate!" Janot pants.

I am breathing in a cadence to keep from passing out behind the rubber boots of Tigre. I am feeling sorry enough for myself as I struggle to keep pace behind the tiger of the mountain. I look back at the film crew hauling their cameras and various batteries and can't help but feel sorry for them.

We stop to redistribute our gear. Abbo helps the camera crew, and distributes their heavy items between his own ruck and the rest of ours.

When our guide sees we have completed our task he sets off once more. The pace reminds me of attending Delta Force Selection. It is a blistering move with weight and dramatic change in elevation. It is not a full out run, but it is not a walk either. More like an endless walking sprint. My quads are exploding from the effort under my ruck and the steep terrain on the backside of the tepui.

Tigre motions there is a waterfall ahead and then we turn right and make a final ascent to the flat top summit.

All told, it has taken us an additional week from the time we left Marc Shaw and Ollie in the Yanomami village.

As a team, we have been following Tigre for two days on foot, with another full day ahead of us for the ascent. When we clear the dense brush and find the waterfall, I have a deep sense of accomplishment. A waypoint is made.

The team takes a much-needed break. We strip off our clothes and immerse ourselves in a pool under the cascading falls.

Janot asks Tigre where we go from here in Spanish. Our guide points up the waterfall.

"You had to ask, Janot," I joke.

After getting back into hiking mode we prepare to follow Tigre and I catch hell from the film crew.

"Marco, you said this was going to be a one day assault on the mountain and back down!"

"Yeah, I agree. This is a dick dragger."

I should have accounted for the fact it would be a one-day assault only for an indigenous guide.

"We're running low on water and food."

"I know...we all are," I say.

The guide says this is our last stretch beyond the waterfall. This is the summit. I do not doubt this in the least.

When I climbed Magualida, and Neblina, I realize all signs are indicating we are not far from the top of this mountain. The brush is thinning and I know from experience the most dramatic waterfalls occur near the summits.

We continue our climb up the mountain and true to form, we make the summit shortly thereafter, absolutely exhausted.

We huddle on what appears the top of the world, congratulating one another.

Down to the south I can see the large sentinel post of Neblina towering like a castle wall over the flat expanse of the Amazonian Biosphere Reserve.

To the west are the expansive western flats, jungles, and rivers of Colombia. It looks like a verdant green form of the ocean itself.

To the north, the giant *tepui* above La Esmeralda stands like another guard tower facing the west. Just beyond that are the sentinel post of Magaulida and the Lost World of the Hoti.

This is it. I am a sentinel on the wall facing west. The wall is what they call The Guiana Shield. For a moment, this all makes sense. This is an amazing adventure. El Tigre points to the trail that leads to the gold mine, and gives me a thumbs up. We are here.

The film crew hands me their sat phone; Sir Peter Blake is on the other end of the line.

"Anything to report, Mr. Lonergan?"

"Sierra Two, top of the world, Capitan! We made it!"

I am slightly premature, but I capture the moment in a phone call.

"Congratulations, mate!" my captain exclaims. *"Just for the record, we also picked up BMW vehicles as a sponsor for the Northwest Passage!"*

"No kidding, Pete?"

"Yes, my friend. You can now have that bush plane you wanted and all the toys you need to pull off another great adventure."

"Awesome! Please pass that on to Ollie and Marc Shaw. Also, please let Doc Fullerton know we are at the rally point and moving to the objective."

"Roger that, mate. Oh, and Mr. Lonergan?"

"Yes, *Capitan?*"

"Keep everyone safe. No one dies on our watch."

"Aye, *Capitan.*"

Almost on cue, an indigenous male and female come climbing up the backside of the trail wearing woven baskets. It could not be a better transition.

"What the fuck iz theeez sheet!" shouts Janot in utter surprise. "We're in the middle of nowhere. What iz theez?"

Tigre greets the couple with enthusiasm and huddles with them on some rocks across from our position overlooking the expanse of the UN Biosphere Reserve. It is a beautiful scene, suddenly turned dramatic.

The air is now much cooler up here and the sweat starts to cool on our bodies. The elevation at the top of Aracamoni is nearly 5,000 feet.

As Janot, Abbo, and the film crew stir with their gear, Tigre shoots me a glance and a signal for us to move ahead.

I point to my eye as a challenge, like I did with the Hoti children. Tigre responds with his hands on his thighs and turns down the trail the couple just walked up from. It drops steeply into a valley.

Janot talks with Alberto and they translate the news that a gold mine is not far below in a small valley. The couple looks extremely worried. We are definitely in the right spot.

Fear starts to crawl up the back of my neck and I give Tigre the signal to take us ahead. We have come a long way to get us here, but I have no idea what awaits us beyond.

I make a group discussion out of the turn of events. It is refreshing to me since I was torturing myself on how I would push the troop ahead.

"Mate, it's almost dark and we have no food. And it's getting cold."

"We either climb down the mountain now or we go forward to the mine."

"We're committed," Alistair charges. "I say we go forward."

Alberto consults with Tigre off to the side in an effort to add some weight to the decision-making process.

"Marco, Tigre says we can make camp there tonight," he reports. "The Cabocles are out, it's just the workers. We'll be okay."

"Thanks, Beto."

"What's that sheet?" asks Janot. The French adventurer is processing our options.

"Beto said it right, gents. We can go ahead and showcase the mine with our cameras. Once we have proof the Venezuela military will come in and shut this whole thing down. We can make a difference right now."

"I'm cold and I'm hungry," Abbo says. "Do you think they will help us?"

"I hope so, Abbo."

"I say we go for it," Janot says. "We need to do theez."

Simon and James watch on and initially object. They are starting to pull out of their roles as filmmakers and go into survival mode.

"I have a bad feeling about this," Simon laments. "I have all day since we've been climbing this mountain."

"Hang with us, Simon. This could get interesting for the film piece."

"All right, we'll film it."

I motion for Tigre to charge ahead down the narrow trail. We notice right away the pieces of rope tied along the steep trail. Alberto tells us it is a handrail for the porters to help them balance the generators and large equipment they are forced to carry back here for the mine.

The trail below is steep and it is creepy. We all have a hard time keeping up with Tigre. He is on a mission.

It is dark by the time we roll into a secluded valley on top of the tepui. The surrounding land is scarred like a battle zone, peppered with a lot of tiny huts constructed out of poles, boards, corrugated tin, and cardboard in places.

We are greeted by several Indians who swarm around Tigre. He moves on down into the camp and we follow him to a hut with ornate blankets for walls. He leads us inside and introduces us to an old woman. She looks Hoti. She has the same bearing as the shaman woman I met in Magualida, and large, caring eyes. She is wearing tattered clothing and has the signature beads crossing her chest. In her ears, she has thread cores as decorations, and a few containers hanging in her beads for powders and mixtures.

In her care are several young children who all appear to be Hoti.

Tigre squats down and opens an embrace to one of the boys. They rock together in a silent embrace as the film crew lumbers in like bulls in a china shop. Janot picks up the exchange with Tigre and pushes the oafs back to create space.

The woman invites all of us to sit in the hut and settles us down next to Tigre and his boy. She cooks us a hot pot of rice.

I take my time and eat my serving slowly. It is one of the most delicious meals I have ever eaten.

Our team settles into the hut and we are given blankets. Others from the mine come up to us and greet us with various bits of food and more blankets. The entire group, including the film crew, are taken by the hospitality we are given.

As I lay to sleep that night, I am overcome by a great sense of accomplishment.

I doze off, exhausted and beaten up.

I wake abruptly, recovering from a fitful sleep. My Omega watch glows 2:30 am. I had a nightmare, and it wasn't the Cabocle miners coming in the camp; it was something else. It is like the old woman from Magualida said, that I am pursued through the jungle by something bad, something following me from the land of the mist and snow to the painted waters of the Amazon.

Something is wrong.

I dream that night of dark shadows and I see a bright light. I have a Guardian watching over me, and over the team I have led into dangerous places. There is a warm and powerful presence with us.

I also have a vivid dream of Sir Peter Blake in a bathtub, pale white. In my dream it is odd to see him this way, and I awake abruptly. I breathe deeply in the cold mountain air of Aracamoni. In the shadows of the hut a candle is burning. Bathed in the flickering orange glow Alberto is sitting watch over us all, shotgun in his lap. Our sentinel.

The next morning we spend the day filming the illegal mine.

The Cabocles who run the camp are down the mountain. Many who are forced to work the mine dare not escape; they just continue to work. It is a surreal experience for all of us.

When they see us up here with the cameras they know that the Guardia Nacional will fly in and arrest or kill the Cabocles. They know their time on the tepui is short. There is a festive environment on the site.

There are workers from Colombia who specialize in water cannons. They have heavy water pumps carried up the mountain, along with a steady supply of fuel. Farther down are the workers in the mines.

As a team, we go down into the shafts, only as wide as three bodies, and watch the miners pick away at veins, tracing them underground by candlelight.

Last, we go to the rivers, where the women and children work by panning the soil in the creek that flows through the center of the camp. It is quite an extensive operation, and sad to see, knowing the story behind many of the workers up here.

Janot does a most poignant piece for the Nat Geo film, where he comments on these workers being normal people, not criminals. I wanted to go into more detail on the effect of the Cabocles and the forced labor and violence that takes place in these mines.

The kidnappings and the killings by the Cabocle miners and illegal timber harvesters are about to get much worse.

It is a reward for me to that know Peter, the crew, and I are all a part of the solution today by making the mine. We are all looking forward to showing Sir Peter the footage.

We spend one more night in the camp.

The next day we make it back down to the dugout with the goods on film and start the long boat ride back to the Casiquiare to meet up with Ollie and Marc Shaw.

We make it back and find Ollie has pretty much adopted the entire village. Little Monk and El Tigre are now gone, and I pray that they are all safe and firmly in God's Hands. Lucho later confirms they are.

We move out of the village for a group camp that night on a sandy white beach.

We spend the night around the campfire telling stories and bonding. It is a good evening with the team, and we discuss doing a crocodile dive on our way down the Casiquiare, in a clear tributary that Lucho knows about.

The next morning when we wake, we get the news.

Ollie is talking into the sat phone and completely distraught. He pulls all of us in down at the expedition vessel and makes a somber announcement.

"Sir Peter Blake is dead."

The blood runs from my face and tears spring to my eyes. The unthinkable has indeed happened.

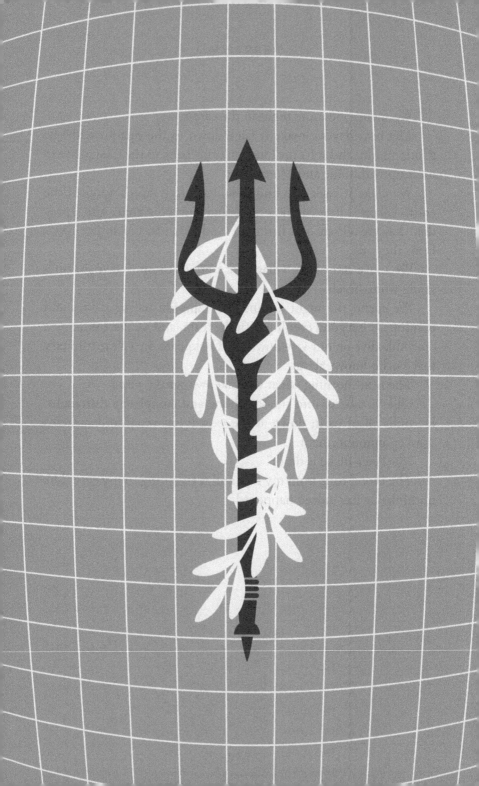

SIR PETER AND THE PIRATES

Macapa, Brazil
05 DECEMBER 2001
AUTHOR AGE: 35

I was able to retrace the events leading to Sir Peter's death from various reports to investigative journalists and the actual deposition to Brazilian authorities by the man who killed my captain. He is now serving a thirty-six-year sentence with one unsuccessful escape attempt. The following is the story as reported from separate sources:

Ricardo Tavares and two of his gang members, Macedo and Cardoso, sit on the beach drinking Antarctica beer and looking out across the muddy beach that the low tide exposes for a moment. It is the afternoon of December 5.

The town is reeling under the fear of the *real* gangs moving up from the south. These guys are in the drug trade, and associated with the cartels.

Fazendinha is known as a beach resort town of sorts. The beach club area has a white sand beach, the only one for miles along this part of the Amazon River.

It is definitely a poor man's Riviera. No one goes there except for employees of the timber trade and the mines of northern Roraima. That and now the drug trade.

Rico and his team had stuck to petty crime up until now. They had hit a few tourist boats that were crazy enough to come down this part of the river.

Usually the tourist boats go in and out of the Amazon River in Belem, far to the south. If for some reason tourists do come to this town instead of Belem, the harbormaster does his job by leading the ships right into Rico's trap.

Early that morning in a tiny wooden shed at Fazendinha, a beachside village 15km west of Macapa, duty Harbormaster Claudio Lira heard about the vessel Seamaster trying to anchor in a river tributary further west near the town of Santana.

Lira got on his Marine band radio and guided Sir Peter and the vessel to an anchorage offshore of the main town near the beach clubs and the rundown brothels. He had no idea the captain was an international figure, a legend in his homeland and across the world.

"Vessel *Seamaster*, I advise you anchor off Fazendinha because it is safer for you than the tributary near Santana," he said.

Seamaster set down its anchor several hundred meters offshore and began preparing for the customs agents to come aboard.

As it did every day in this part of the world, straddling the equator, the sun set about 6 pm, stranding *Seamaster* in the pitch black. The crew decided to indulge in a meal on shore before dark to celebrate the expedition and the fact that they were due to slip out of the Amazon the next day and cruise up the coast towards Venezuela for the rendezvous with the Jungle Team.

The captain and the sailing crew beached the rubber Zodiac boat on the sandy shoreline of the "resort area" of Fazendinha, and walked up to Bar du Bizerra, a hole-in-the-wall like the others along the beach, with tables and chairs spreading over the road and onto the sand.

Tavares and his two young companions could not be more astonished by the apparition of the large, bulbous polar vessel off the shore. They watch the yacht's crew come ashore to drink and make phone calls.

Just before dark, the crew returns to the yacht.

Tavares and his gang of three watch them come and go in the black inflatable propelled to high speeds by a large outboard motor.

On their return to *Seamaster*, most of the crew sit on the back deck enjoying a few cans of beer.

Tavares, Macedo, and Cardoso leave the bar and find three other men in the nearby village of Santana: Isael da Costa, whose 27th birthday is the next day; Isael's brother Josué da Costa, 29; and Rubens Souza, 20.

In Macapá, there is almost no twilight; night falls fast. Since the yacht looked like it was staying put for the evening, they decide to head out to it in a *catraia*, a fishing boat with an outboard, and stick up the crew. They go to Rico's house to eat dinner and collect what they need for the night's mission.

When they move to the river's edge just before 9 pm, four of them pull on motorcycle helmets and the other two don balaclava-like hoods. Tavares, Cardoso, and Isael da Costa carry handguns. They get into the *catraia* and motor out into the river, then paddle noiselessly as they near the boat. The pirates hear music coming from the well-lit stern. No one is on watch. They are oblivious to the pirates approaching just off her stern in the oily smooth surface of the Amazon River.

Aboard *Seamaster*, Sir Peter Blake finishes up writing in his captain's log down below deck in his office. He is writing his final entries before departing the river for the Atlantic Ocean.

Pete writes a passage in his log that reflects on making our objectives:

"My racing days are now complete. I don't have that fire anymore. But a new fire is even stronger, and I guess we have all closed in again to the point where we want the same thing as a team, to make a difference in how people perceive and understand the wonders and needs of the environment that surrounds us."

Sir Peter's log also records a forlorn reference to how much he missed his family: "I know I spend too much time away from my family. But that is the life we have chosen."

Outside Sir Peter's door, Rubens da Silva Souza, the 20-year-old local, eases the rickety launch towards *Seamaster* with his band of pirates. In their eyes, this boat is a prime target for robbery. They presume it is a boatload of millionaires on holiday. Between them they have a formidable record of these crimes and don't expect to encounter any resistance.

With military precision, they storm the boat and almost immediately discover these crew members have more fight in them than anyone they had ever come across. Up on deck, one bandit rushes towards crew member Rodger Moore, Alistair's dad. Moore responds by throwing his beer can at his face. The robber lashed out with his firearm, whacking Moore across the face and leaving him with a black eye.

Down below decks Sir Peter hears a scramble on the fantail of the vessel. His instinct is to protect his crew, some of whom are being forced to cower on the deck outside. He hears them shouting, and the shouts in Portuguese. His chef, Paulo, runs past his office shouting "Pirates!" in English, then starts shouting in Portuguese again to try to quell any language barrier.

Pete heads to his cabin and digs out the soft case containing a .308 caliber hunting rifle, exactly where I left it so many months ago. Earlier in the journey, it was my responsibility to handle ship security. I made a point of cleaning and lubricating the rifle, I even polished and lubricated each round in the small ammunition clip mounted below the receiver. The weapon was only onboard because of polar bears, when the vessel travelled to the North in its earlier life with its builder and captain, Jean Luis Etienne. I was the only crew member who handled the weapon, and tragically never taught my captain how to properly handle the beast. It is not a close quarters combat weapon, like the Ithaca shotgun I saw on the pirates of Dolphin Island with Katia. This is a long range, bolt-action hunting rifle with a large caliber round, capable of penetrating any of the topside bulkheads of *Seamaster* like butter. This means a bullet fired from this weapon will travel through walls, even after exiting a human body. This makes firing the weapon on the ship very dangerous to bad guys as well as our crew. My only speech to the captain was that I would use it only as a last resort, and ideally to hold armed attackers at a distance from the vessel. My experiences earlier on the riverboat in Manaus with a rusty pistol and the children, never left my mind while Miguel and I were onboard *Seamaster* together with the team. I should have told them all the story; it might have saved lives.

I know from my experience with Sir Peter, in the captain's mind, it is now his responsibility to guard the crew.

Sir Peter Blake makes a fatal choice.

Outside of his cabin, Leon Sefton, one of the expedition crew onboard, is in his cabin directly across from him. He is waking up from a nap, rushing to put on a pair of surf trunks to see what the fuss is all about.

Out of the corner of his eye, Pete observes a hooded pirate enter the passageway from the stern and put a pistol to Leon's head, forcing the Kiwi to take a knee.

The man yells, "Money, money, money!!!" in broken English.

Pete pulls the weapon out, grabs the charging handle of the bolt carrier group, rotates upward, and pulls it back.

A long brass cartridge is exposed in the magazine and pops up to line itself into the chamber. He charges the bolt forward and locks it in, thumb off the safety, and puts the weapon on fire.

Sir Peter Blake charges out of his cabin with the loaded weapon and runs face to face with the masked pirate named Da Costa.

"Right, get the fuck off my boat!" the captain shouts.

Shocked, the pirate backpedals into the main salon and raises his pistol with his left hand. He fires two rounds; they go wide, missing the captain and Leon.

Sir Peter fires and the bullet goes through two of Da Costa's left fingers, blowing the pistol out of his hand and onto the deck of the salon.

The fingers fall onto the deck near the galley. Sir Peter fires another round at the man and the bullet strikes Da Costa's forearm and lodges near his elbow.

The pirate runs back to the stairwell, up to the fantail toward his leader, screaming in pain. Two of his fingers are lying back on the deck of the galley. The leader of the pirate gang reacts by heading down the stairs toward the captain.

Down below, Sir Peter attempts to reload the weapon with a third round from the magazine. Everything hits him at once.

Leon approaches the captain. "You want more bullets, Pete?" he asks, motioning back to the bandolier I had loaded, now sitting on Pete's bunk.

Pete motions him to the bow. "Clear the fan from the forward hatch and get the boys ready to get up on the bow if we have to. Keep the boys safe!"

"You're a brave bastard, Pete!" Leon yells to his captain.

Sir Peter forces the semi-open bolt forward, but the third round jams between the bolt, the magazine, and the chamber. He did not pull the bolt back far enough to the rear to strip the round from the magazine below and guide it into its berth within the chamber properly. To clear it is a practiced method called: Tap. Rack. Bang. All gunfighters know the drill. Sir Peter is not a gunfighter.

He hears the shouting above deck from his crew fighting the pirates, and Da Costa's screams. Footsteps are shuffling on the other side of the wall.

Sir Peter gets frustrated with the weapon. It is not cooperating. With the charging spirit of a man who has raced and survived across 300,000 miles of ocean, the captain refuses to give up easily. He resorts to the only thing he can think of at the time.

He slams the weapon's stock against the deck and frees the cartridge.

While he is doing that, Ricardo Tavares walks down the stairwell behind the captain.

He observes the man slamming the weapon on the deck near the cooking area of the ship. The tall man with the bushy blond hair is wearing a white tank top with the word Blakexpeditions written on it in blue letters on his back. He does not know the pirate is behind him. Ricardo raises his pistol and fires one round.

The bullet pierces Sir Peter's left scapula, smashes through his lung, and cuts through his aorta. Tavares fires a second bullet that pierces the captain's left scapula again, and ends up in his armpit.

The pirate runs below and grabs Peter's rifle, then strips the Omega Seamaster watch from his wrist while he is still breathing.

Clutching cameras, lenses, watches, and money they had stolen, the robbers tie the black Zodiac to the back of their motorboat and zoom off into the night.

They fire indiscriminately, narrowly avoiding killing another crew member, grazing the top of his back with a bullet.

In the galley, Leon Sefton runs back to Sir Peter after hearing the shots when he was up in the bow with the boys. The captain is lying in a pool of blood on the galley floor.

Leon flips him over, and blood pours from his captain's mouth. Sir Peter Blake is ghost white in the recess of the galley. He is dead.

Running up on deck, Leon grabs Paulo, the Brazilian cook, and the two men launch another one of Seamaster's inflatables. They speed ashore and pull harbormaster Lira from a soccer game he is watching.

Lira phones for help, alerting two local launch owners, including one who takes a doctor and local firefighters out to *Seamaster* to help.

There is nothing they can do. Sir Peter Blake is no longer in this world.

Marc and Ollie

Janot

COLOMBIA

VENEZUELA

National Guard Base

ORINOCO RIVER

PUERTO AYACUCHO

ESCAPE ORINOCO

Venezuela / Colombia Border
DECEMBER 2001
AUTHOR AGE: 35

"Lonergan...phone for you!" Ollie yells out to me on the bow of *Seamaster II*. The first mate hands me the sat phone.

"Marco, it's Doc."

"Doc, thanks for calling. I'm doing okay, but this is bone-crushing."

"I called your parents and let them know you are all right. This is going to be coming out in the news."

"Thanks, Doc."

"I told your mom I'll fly out there myself and land a platoon of SEALs to extract you if I need to."

"Thanks, Doc." I know he is not exaggerating.

"Okay, back to the mission, Marco. You have to get that team out of there. No more accidents."

"Huh?"

"Sir Peter made a bad call facing off with those guys. He should have pushed them along, not shot at them. I heard the long gun jammed."

"Yeah, Doc. I loaded it."

"Did you clean that fucker?"

"Yeah, Doc. I freaking polished every round and had the sheath set for a quick draw."

"Did you have a round loaded in the chamber?"

"No, bolt locked forward, four rounds in the clip, weapon on safe."

"Did you teach him how to load it?"

"No."

"You shouldn't have been flashing that weapon in his face. You planted a bad seed in his brain."

"I know, Doc."

"Fuck, Marcus."

"Aye, Senior Chief."

"Here's the deal. I was telling your captain that the FARC on the Colombian side of the Orinoco is kicked up in a frenzy. No bullshit— all stop. Also, our guy Lucho has been stealing from the fuel cache out of Tama-Tama and running it into Colombia, we cannot trust him to take you along the Colombian border alone."

"What's up?"

"They are starting a counter-FARC mission with the US called PLAN COLOMBIA..."

"Oh shit."

"My preference is for you to fly your guys out from La Esmeralda. That's what I was telling Pete before he got shot."

"Okay, Doc. I'll talk to the team."

"I have Jonathan Gilliam and Andy helping me sort some contacts out for you with a Venezuelan commander in theater where I am getting my intel."

"Tell the guys I said thanks, Doc."

"No need. Just make it happen with the team and we'll talk soon. I can make arrangements to have a helo out there if you need it."

"Roger."

I hang up the phone and face off with Ollie. "Ollie, I don't want to throw our guys into a panic, but Doc is suggesting we fly everyone out at La Esmeralda."

Ollie is completely pale. "I'll talk to the team. You sit here and take a breather, mate."

Ollie goes back to the group and the exchange brings out significant emotions with the team.

This clearly isn't a SEAL Team mission where guys rub dirt in their wounds and distribute ammo to the living members of the ambushed patrol.

The conversation leads to a full on mutiny of me leading this expedition.

Janot walks up to me first. "Hey, don't take this too hard on yourself, mate. Nothing you could do out here."

"I know, Janot. I should have made sure he came with us on the Jungle Team. What we did on Aracamoni was important to him."

"He was proud of us for taking out the mine, yes?"

"He was."

"Good. Then we accomplished our mission on the mountain. I know that for a fact, my friend."

"Well it's important we carry on the mission for Sir Peter, mate. We can't fly out in Esmeralda."

"What?"

"We have to finish this. We have to take this all the way to the mouth of the Orinoco like we planned."

"It's too dangerous."

"We don't think so, mate."

"Fuck, Janot. This is dangerous talk."

"I don't know what you're talking about with your buddy Doc, or what you guys were talking about with Pete, but we want to finish what we started with him."

"I understand, Janot."

The Frenchman is the dedicated spokesman for the group. Ollie discharged the duties to Janot, as I read in his face. He is over it...done.

Alistair is writhing in agony over such a tragic loss and the fact that his father was literally caught in the crossfire.

We got further word that the pirates stole all the crew's Omega watches as well as my black Zodiac. They fired their pistols at

Seamaster as they drove the boat away and several of the crew were hit, fortunately with only grazing wounds.

Alistair's father is all right, but Abbo is inconsolable.

Right now Janot and I are hashing out a mission to extract.

I walk into the group and effectively put out a peace pipe.

"We need to have a plan to get home. As of now, the expedition is over, we just need to get out safely."

Marc Shaw bristles with a strong sense of duty. "We need to keep going!"

I register it and carefully regulate my tone after hurting his feelings and his pride by keeping him back at the Yanomami settlement. I respect his passion for this mission. But he and the others have no idea how dangerous the Orinoco River can be along the Colombian border, even at the best of times.

I have years of experience back here. They do not.

We fly Ollie and Abbo out by seaplane when we get to Tama-Tama to refuel. Abbo flies on to Brazil to meet his dad, and Ollie flies to Caracas to help sort out rental cars from Puerto Ayacucho. At my fuel cache I confirm the missing fuel drums. We have just enough fuel to get home, nothing more.

We drive on to the military base.

In the late hours of the next evening we approach the sandy beaches of San Fernando. It is a creepy evening. The fog on the river is setting slightly above the water and the wind is perfectly still. There are no bugs or birds to be heard. Only the thumping music coming from the Colombian town called Amanaven.

The twins each have the outboard motors on idle as we drift silently around the bend of the river after navigating a labyrinth of sandbars and rocks.

The large sandy beaches around San Fernando have a dull glow in the moonless night.

I know from Doc all we have to do is round the bend and twist into a sandy cove as soon as we are across the river from Colombia.

Doc made arrangements for us to pull into the cove tonight and there will be soldiers expecting us on the beach. Pulling into the base without invitation could be a ticket to getting shot. All our nerves are on edge.

We skirt an inside island and Lucho guides us into the cove.

I have a red lens flashlight I burn on the bow of the vessel as we pull into the cove. We are greeted with an answering red lens light, and I flash in response.

Challenge and reply complete, as per Doc's orders, we beach the boat and I greet the crew on the beach. It is a little intimidating seeing the camouflaged men with armed machine guns for the crew.

To me, it is like coming home, especially in dangerous times.

I am guided alone up to the commander's office. I enter his room and I am reminded of Command Master Chief Chalker when I showed up for BUD/S.

Here I am a scruffy river rat, months in the jungle. I look a mess.

The commander first looks at me and I expect him to say, "Son, you have ten seconds to explain yourself…." Instead, I get a big smile. "You have good people looking out for you, Marco."

"Glad you know my name, sir."

"Quite an adventure you are on. Sorry about your captain."

"Yes, sir."

"Doc Fullerton did a good job keeping me aware of your work back here."

"Aye, sir."

"You guys stumble on the mine up on Aracamoni?"

"Yes, sir. We ended up filming it."

"I heard that will be some work for us. What were they like up there? Indios?"

"Good people, sir. Please take it easy on the Indios in the summit camp up there. It is the miners who are the ones causing the trouble. They have a camp two clicks south of the mine from what I hear."

"You are lucky you lost no more friends than you have. I heard about Dante."

"Yes, sir. He was a good man. Lucho over there is a little sketchy though."

"You need an escort to Puerto Ayacucho."

"Is that a question, sir?"

"No, it is an order."

"Thank you, sir. Much appreciated."

"Marco, these guys down here will skin you alive if they pick you up on the river. You have a couple of days' travel."

"Yes, sir."

"I can give you two Piranha gunboats as escorts. But there's one catch."

"What's that, sir?"

"You have to supply the fuel for our boats. I understand you have a cache up here, *is there any fuel left?*"

"True, sir, but it was compromised up in Tama-Tama by Lucho, I think he was running our gas out to Colombia behind my back. We have just enough to float back to PA ourselves."

"This is a problem, Marco. I warned Doc about Lucho recently. He is a known smuggler up here, I do not like him. It is best we stay close to you on the border, there is no telling who he was supplying."

"I had a feeling." I motion outside and pull out my sat phone. "Let me step outside and make a call, sir."

I call my First Mate. "Ollie, baby!"

"Marco! I got Abbo out to Brazil. Getting flights lined up for us, and just took a hot shower, mate!" Ollie sounds happy on the other end of the line. It is nice to hear some cheer in his voice.

"Way to rub it in, Ollie. I have a favor to ask."

"What's up, mate?"

"Can you be waiting for us in Puerto Ayacucho with the rental vehicles and, say, two fifty gallon drums of fuel?"

"How long do I have?"

"Two days."

"Okay, mate. I'll be there."

"Cheers, Ollie. And put away the mermaid dollars."

"Piss off, mate."

As the sun rises above the Guiana Shield to the east, I sit on the bow of the catamaran *Seamaster II* and take in the warm breeze of the Rio Orinoco. To my front and to my rear I am flanked to the west by two Venezuelan Army gunboats. The base commander takes a big chance with me. I promise him Ollie will be at the dock when we pull into town. He has enough fuel for his boats to make the trip one way. If I come up short he will be stuck in town and without two of his most important boats away from his base.

It is a huge risk for him.

This is the magic of Doc Fullerton in full bloom. There is no way I could navigate back here without his support for this run.

Sir Peter was aware enough to fully recognize the fact that he did not just get one expedition team member, but an entire SEAL Team at his disposal.

It is sad we did not have a contingency for him to be in Brazil and separated by so many miles.

I sit next to Janot with the protective spirit of Sir Peter over our shoulders and smiling, of this I am sure.

The gunboat crews are in great spirits and turn up some loud music on their PA system.

It is the soundtrack from *Apocalypse Now*, the "The Ride of the Valkyries." The music selection could not be better.

We cruise south on the Orinoco for two days, as planned. When we arrive in Puerto Ayacucho at a sandy beach at the end of a makeshift boat ramp and a small pier we are greeted by Ollie. He is sitting on two fuel drums side by side.

He's wearing a Hawaiian shirt and has real dollar bills stuffed in his pockets for the boat crews and their commander, and a big bottle of whiskey.

Mission accomplished.

For all the sadness that has ensued over the past several days, we have a brief respite of healing knowing that Sir Peter Blake is with us all, smiling and joining us for a rum and Coke.

The film crew heads off with Jefe back to Caracas to document their footage and submit forms on the gold mine piece for government review and approvals.

I call Doc Fullerton from the dock and let him know we are okay, and I thank my friends back at SEAL Team Four Headquarters.

The camaraderie continues beyond active duty with the teams. In all the branches of service and all the Special Operations Commands I interacted with, none of them capture something as unique as what the Navy SEALs have.

I can't put my finger on what exactly it is, but I do know our deep bond with the ocean, the silent world, plays a strong part in this brotherhood of warriors, both in peace and in war.

Following our wake for Sir Peter in Auckland, I say goodbye to my friends and start on the path back home a changed man.

The greatest change for me is the realization of the calling for a higher purpose than self. That the greatest reward comes from risking one's life for a purpose greater than self, for man and nature, all things great and small.

As Sir Peter would say, "Why bother? Because it is the very essence of our existence as protectors."

WAR

THE PHONE CALL
Newport, Rhode Island
AUTUMN 2003
AUTHOR AGE: 37

After Sir Peter's death, the Cousteau Society has me developing an Advanced Diving Lab at the University of Rhode Island. The dean of the Ocean Engineering department got me a room in a historic house in old town Newport near the shipyard. The house comes with a female Italian chef as a roommate named Grace.

One morning I am awakened by my cellphone going off in my ear.

"Hello?"

"Marc, my name is Brian. I know you from the SEAL Teams."

"Cool, brother."

"Doc Fullerton told me to give you a call."

"Now I know you mean trouble. What's up, Brian?"

"I'm a former Master Chief over at DEVGRU. I have a challenge for you."

"No shit?"

"You show up down here at the training site in North Carolina tomorrow morning and take a shooting test. If you pass you will not be working for the military, you will be working for the secret squirrels. Doc tells me you're a great shot."

"I can shoot, but I'm up in Rhode Island," I reply, slightly defensive.

"Showtime is 0800. Pass this test and it will change your life," he *tells me.*

"Roger, Master Chief, I'll be there."

What the hell have I just done?

I haven't fired a weapon in three years since getting out of the Teams. I am totally screwed.

I will never forget the night when a warm breeze entered the windows of the old house and I made a comment to Grace. I saw a light flick in through the window, race across the wall of her bedroom, and into mine in the upstairs of the house.

"Winds of change, Grace. I feel it," I said to her as she laid in her soft white sheets and blankets.

The next day, *Seamaster* pulled into the Newport shipyard. It was by completely by chance that I was living in view of her new berth.

The owner of the shipyard, Charlie Dana, gave her free moorage at his docks since he was such a good friend of Sir Peter.

Ollie and Janot sailed her up with a helper crew.

All this was completely unknown or announced between us.

Imagine the look on my face to see Janot and Ollie below my window, of all the places on the planet for *Seamaster* to be berthed!

I jump out of bed. My bare feet hit the warm wooden floors of my upstairs bedroom. This old house was built in the 1700s and is in immaculate condition.

I prop open my window on a warm summer morning and look out to the Newport Harbor at the rigging of the sailboats over at Newport shipyard. The gentle breeze knocks and rattles the lines that run up their masts.

I pick out a particular twang and rattle of an aluminum mast that strikes a chord in me, like the sound of a familiar song played on a baby grand piano.

I follow the notes to the tall rigging of *Seamaster*. We are all together again. It is spooky.

I see stirring on top of her deck and recognize the shapes darting about in their daily chores.

"Ollie! Janot! You guys want breakfast?"

"Marcoooooooo!!" Ollie responds. "Hell yeah! We'll be right there, mate!"

The beautiful, spritely figure of the Italian chef and professional yacht photographer named Grace Trofa is working away in a most beautiful kitchen.

The sun is rising into the wooden framed windows and illuminating her basil plants on the sill. Grace already has fresh tomatoes chopped and eggs cooking on the large, open-faced stove.

I walk downstairs and greet my friends. We share a wonderful meal together.

Yes, there is magic in this life.

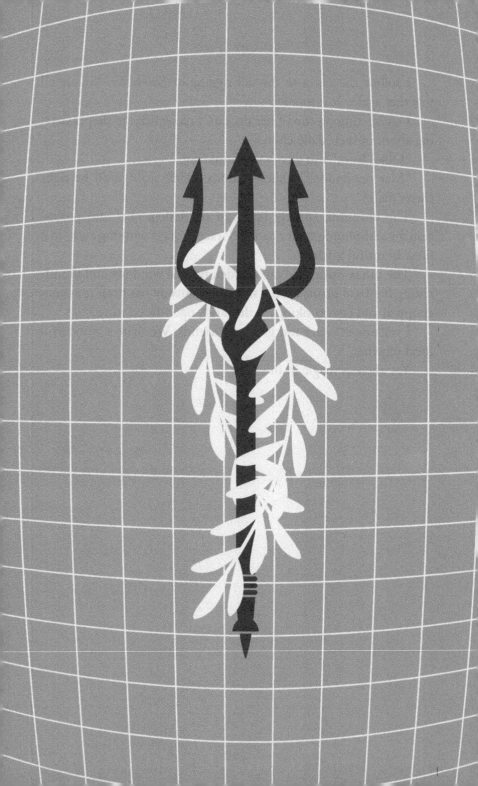

THE SHOOTING TEST

North Carolina
AUTUMN 2003
AUTHOR AGE: 37

"Welcome to the training site. State your business," the guard at the gate greets me.

"I'm here for the shooting test."

"You're on the list?"

"Yes, Brian invited me to show up."

"You're Hur-tell?" he asks.

"Yep."

"You're late, dude. They're about to start."

"He said 0800. It's, like, 0730?"

"Heads up, killer. Always show up an hour early."

"Where do I go?"

"Go to the main lodge and park. The armory is in the back. Look up John Carswell, he'll issue your weapons."

"Cool, thanks."

"Yeah, good luck. It's a tough test, man."

Ughhhhh

What am I getting myself into? I navigate several miles down a flat tree-lined road through the large training facility one of my former teammates built.

On the drive down, Doc Fullerton calls me and gives me some pointers.

The test is to handpick a special group of operators for a team working directly under the president of the United States. The official mission is to support US government initiatives in Iraq for Operation Iraqi Freedom.

The list of invitees for the test is impressive; the number of slots available is small.

I am once again faced with a challenge.

I only have the years of experience I built in my earlier years to lean back on for this one. As a former sniper, I know one thing I do possess: excellent muscle memory. I remember the feel of a well-placed weapon cradled into my cheek, sight alignment, and proper sight picture. Instinctively know my breathing and the feeling of steady pressure on a cold metal trigger.

"Marco!" I turn to see an old friend from my SEAL Team days, John Carswell.

"Johnny C! Haven't seen you since we trained out here with Charlie Platoon. How goes it?"

"Good, Marco. Welcome back. Here's your weapons. You better get out there, it's about to start."

"Fuck, I'm always showing up for these things at the last minute!"

"Well, you better zero this long gun in quick time. I have no idea if it's sighted in."

The M4 carbine he hands me has a scopelike sight on it that I have never seen.

"What the fuck is this thing?"

"It's an Eotech sight. It has a bright red reticle inside. Zero it in at fifty yards. Your test will run from the one hundred down to the ten."

"Oh shit."

I take the M4 carbine and a 9mm Sig-Sauer P226 over to the firing range where a bunch of snake eaters are lining up.

I see a berm with a wooden table and another SEAL looking dude standing next to it getting ready to move out to the range.

"Dude, how do you work this Eotech?" I ask the blond hair and chiseled chin.

"Oh you're fucked," he answers.

He starts to walk off, then turns around, calling back, "Adjust your elevation and windage here. Zero here on the fifty into the berm. Here's a mag with three rounds."

"Thanks!"

I quickly dial in the weapons sling and fire one round downrange from the offhand position into a silhouette target fifty yards away from me.

I can barely make out the impact as high and to the right. It is a good shot.

I make my adjustments.

I fire another round. The impact on the target is center bull's-eye but right three inches.

I make my adjustment.

Third round, I punch the black.

I glance to my right and find the man with the chiseled chin is staring at me.

"Nice group. My name is Ty. Let's go. We'll show up to the line together."

"Right on. I'm Marco."

"I don't recognize you from DevGroup."

"I'm from Team Four."

"Oh, did Doc send you?" he asks as we approach the live range.

"Yeah."

"He's a good dude. He'll be running this program one day."

"Yeah, that's Doc. Let's crush this one, brother."

At the line is a bunch of instructors, all wearing long sleeve civilian shirts and all with a distinctive look. They are the men from a secret site that I attended long ago to train as a Force Recon Marine, long before the SEALs.

I am home.

The test consists of us starting way back at the 100-yard line from sitting, to kneeling, to standing with the M4. We are allotted a certain amount of rounds and required to fire them in a timed manner and halted with the sound of a beeping timer.

We finish shooting at the specific yard line and move closer and repeat the course of fire.

We move closer, then move from firing the long gun to transition drills with the pistol. Drop a round out of black on the way down the drill and you are out, thanks for coming.

We get to the final round and the instructors go down the line after the line is cold. As the instructor views your target he gives you a thumbs up to stay and down to get the fuck out.

The firing line started some forty strong. We are down to twenty odd.

The instructors load fresh targets on the stands for the ones that remain. This time the bull's eye is smaller.

Same drill. Back to the hundred yard line. Smaller black, don't drop a round.

"Shooters you have thirty seconds to fire ten rounds in the off-hand position. Reeaddyyyyyy."

BEEEEEEP

One thousand one, one thousand two, one thousannnd... POW!

One thousand one...one thousand two...POW!

One thousand one...one thousand two...POW!

I move down the firing lines, still alive with a thumbs up at the end.

Now there are twelve men.

Smaller targets.

Ugggghhhh, this is killin' me.

In the end, I shake Ty's hand and pat a handful of others on the back.

My new team.

THE JOURNEY EAST

Beirut, Lebanon, to Amman, Jordan
YEAR: 2003
AUTHOR AGE: 37

I board the commercial aircraft and find my window seat near the front of the plane.

Fortunately, the center seat is empty, and even more fortunate, the aisle seat is occupied by a woman wearing a large red scarf. She looks up at me. All I notice are her brown eyes and the bright red scarf wrapped around her golden hair. Her eyes are full of life, but she looks very tired.

The woman is younger than me, maybe in her mid-twenties. She curls her legs up onto her seat and I get settled into my space.

"My name is Marco. Nice to meet you."

"I'm Maria," she says.

"You remind me of Rapunzel," I say jokingly, although I wasn't.

"What's up with the body armor?" she asks.

"It's too important to check. Are you flying to Jordan?" I ask her.

Our destination on the aircraft is scheduled for Amman today.

"I'm going where you're going by the looks of it," she says coyly.

"Really?"

"Yeah, I have a nonprofit that looks out for children caught in conflicts."

"Wow, that sounds like dangerous stuff."

"It is for the children."

"Amen, Maria. I learned some lessons from the orphans of Brazil, I think of it as leaving behind golden footprints where we travel."

We end up talking for quite a while during the flight.

At some point of our journey she curls up in her chair and weeps, resting her head on my left arm, eventually falling asleep.

I put my hand on her red scarf and feel the heat from her head travel all the way to my soul. I hold her as she cries.

She is a very powerful spirit.

Before we split up at the airport in Amman, Jordan, I give her a big hug and get her contact information. She tells me she is staying at the Al Hamra Hotel in Baghdad.

I make it a mission to find her some personal body armor and deliver it to her in Iraq. I may be able to help her in her endeavors as a guardian of the innocent trapped within a war zone.

It will be a mission that I will not fail. I get goosebumps thinking about Sir Peter Blake and our mission together, and the importance of it continuing—in this life and the next.

I just found Sierra Two, and it is cradled between the two rivers of ancient Mesopotamia, and a woman I refer to as an Angel of Baghdad.

She will enter my life again. We are traveling on the same path.

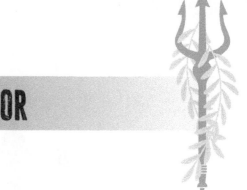

ABOUT THE AUTHOR

Marc Lonergan-Hertel is a former Navy SEAL sniper and professional explorer. His adventure programs have been televised across the world with National Geographic Channel and Discovery Channel. Marc also worked in classified government programs in Iraq in support of Operation Iraqi Freedom.